Blockchain Mastery: Building Decentralized Applications from Beginner to Expert

Kameron Hussain and Frahaan Hussain

Published by Kameron Hussain, 2025.

BLOCKCHAIN MASTERY: BUILDING DECENTRALIZED APPLICATIONS FROM BEGINNER TO EXPERT

First edition. April 6, 2025.

ISBN: 979-8227514615

Written by Kameron Hussain and Frahaan Hussain.

Blockchain Mastery:

FIRST EDITION

BUILDING DECENTRALIZED APPLICATIONS FROM BEGINNER TO EXPERT

Preface

Blockchain technology has become one of the most transformative innovations of the modern digital era. Initially popularized by cryptocurrencies such as Bitcoin, blockchain has rapidly evolved, influencing a myriad of industries beyond finance, from supply chain logistics to decentralized social platforms. This book, *Introduction to Blockchain and Decentralized Applications (DApps)*, serves as a comprehensive guide for developers, technologists, and entrepreneurs looking to navigate this rapidly expanding field.

Organized systematically, the chapters progress from foundational concepts to advanced development techniques, providing the reader with a robust understanding of blockchain and decentralized application development. Whether you're new to blockchain technology or an experienced developer aiming to expand your expertise into DApp development, this book aims to offer practical insights and clear guidance.

The early chapters establish a strong foundation, explaining blockchain architecture, fundamental cryptographic principles, and consensus mechanisms, ensuring readers are comfortable with core concepts before proceeding to practical development techniques. Readers will find clear guidance on setting up development environments, mastering Solidity and other smart contract languages, and building both backend and frontend components of fully functional DApps.

In the latter half, advanced concepts such as Layer 2 solutions, cross-chain interoperability, and decentralized governance are explored, equipping readers with the knowledge to build sophisticated, scalable, and secure DApps. Real-world case studies, including DeFi platforms, NFT marketplaces, and enterprise blockchain applications, bridge theory with practical implementation, highlighting successful applications of blockchain technology in various industries.

Finally, the book discusses emerging trends and future innovations, offering insights into how technologies like Web3, zero-knowledge proofs, and blockchain-AI integration will shape the digital economy of tomorrow.

It is my hope that this book will not only serve as a comprehensive resource but also inspire you to innovate, build, and contribute meaningfully to the exciting and ever-evolving blockchain ecosystem.

Table of Contents

Blockchain

Block Explorer

Block Reward

Consensus Mechanism

Cryptocurrency

DAO (Decentralized Autonomous Organization)

DApp (Decentralized Application)

DeFi (Decentralized Finance)

Double Spending

EIP (Ethereum Improvement Proposal)

EVM (Ethereum Virtual Machine)

Fork

Gas

Gas Fee

Hash

Hash Rate

ICO (Initial Coin Offering)

Interoperability

Layer 2 Scaling

Liquidity

Mainnet

Merkle Tree

Miner

Mining

NFT (Non-Fungible Token)

Node

Off-Chain

On-Chain

Oracle

P2P (Peer-to-Peer)

Private Key

Proof of Stake (PoS)

Proof of Work (PoW)

Public Key

Rug Pull

Satoshi

Smart Contract

Testnet

Token

Tokenomics

NFT and Web3 Questions

Conclusion

Chapter 1: Introduction to Blockchain and Decentralized Applications (DApps)

Understanding Blockchain Technology

BLOCKCHAIN TECHNOLOGY has rapidly become a cornerstone of innovation, fundamentally reshaping how we approach transactions, data management, and trust in digital ecosystems. At its simplest, a blockchain is a decentralized, distributed ledger designed to record transactions across multiple computers securely and transparently. However, beneath this simple definition lies a complex ecosystem of cryptographic methods, consensus protocols, and decentralized architectures, each meticulously designed to solve long-standing issues in traditional digital and economic systems.

What Is Blockchain?

BLOCKCHAIN IS ESSENTIALLY a digital ledger composed of blocks that securely record transactions. Each block contains a set of transactions, timestamped and cryptographically secured, linked sequentially to preceding blocks through a cryptographic hash. This structure ensures the integrity and immutability of data, making any alterations practically impossible without consensus from the majority of network participants.

The Structure of Blockchain

A BLOCKCHAIN IS FORMED through interconnected blocks. Each block consists of:

- **Block Header**: Contains metadata including a timestamp, a nonce (number used only once), and the cryptographic hash of the previous block.
- **Transaction Data**: A record of transactions validated by network participants.

For example, a simplified version of a block structure could be represented as:

```
{
"blockNumber": 101,
"previousHash": "0000000000000000a1b2c3d4e5f67890...",
"timestamp": 1624655000,
"nonce": 2894519,
"transactions": [
{
"sender": "address1",
"recipient": "address2",
"amount": 0.5
},
{
"sender": "address3",
"recipient": "address4",
```

```
"amount": 2.0
}
]
}
```

This cryptographic linking between blocks provides security against unauthorized modifications, as altering a single transaction would invalidate all subsequent blocks.

Decentralization: The Core Principle

BLOCKCHAIN'S REVOLUTIONARY potential stems largely from decentralization—the distribution of control and governance across a network rather than a single entity. In traditional centralized systems, power rests with a single authority, such as a bank, government, or tech giant. In contrast, blockchain disperses power, significantly reducing risks such as censorship, fraud, or systemic failures.

Decentralization manifests itself through various mechanisms:

- **Distributed Ledger**: Every network participant (node) maintains a copy of the ledger, ensuring transparency and redundancy.

- **Consensus Mechanisms**: Nodes collectively agree on the validity of transactions without relying on a trusted intermediary.

- **Peer-to-Peer (P2P) Network**: Information propagates directly among peers, eliminating centralized points of failure.

Cryptographic Foundations

BLOCKCHAIN RELIES HEAVILY on cryptographic techniques to maintain security and privacy. The primary cryptographic concepts utilized include:

Hashing: A cryptographic hash function converts data of arbitrary length into a fixed-length string of characters. It is irreversible and unique, crucial for ensuring data integrity. A commonly used hash function is SHA-256.

Example hashing in Python:

```
python

import hashlib

data = "Blockchain technology"

hash_result = hashlib.sha256(data.encode()).hexdigest()

print(f"Hash: {hash_result}")
```

-

- **Public-Key Cryptography**: A cryptographic method involving a pair of keys—public and private. The public key is used to encrypt data or verify digital signatures, while the private key decrypts data or creates signatures, ensuring secure communication and verification.

Consensus Algorithms

CONSENSUS MECHANISMS ensure agreement on the blockchain's state among distributed nodes. Popular consensus algorithms include:

- **Proof of Work (PoW)**: Used by Bitcoin and early Ethereum implementations, requiring computational effort (mining) to validate transactions and add blocks.

- **Proof of Stake (PoS)**: Validators are chosen based on their stake (number of coins held), reducing energy consumption compared to PoW.

- **Delegated Proof of Stake (DPoS)**: Token holders delegate their validation power to trusted nodes, providing efficiency and scalability.

Types of Blockchains

BLOCKCHAINS VARY SIGNIFICANTLY based on permission models:

- **Public Blockchains**: Open to anyone, decentralized, secure, and transparent. Example: Bitcoin, Ethereum.

- **Private Blockchains**: Restricted access, controlled by an organization or consortium, offering greater privacy and control. Example: Hyperledger Fabric, Corda.

Applications of Blockchain Technology

BLOCKCHAIN TECHNOLOGY has diverse applications extending far beyond cryptocurrency:

- **Finance and Payments**: Facilitates fast, secure, and cost-efficient peer-to-peer transactions and cross-border payments.

- **Supply Chain Management**: Enhances traceability and transparency, allowing real-time tracking of goods and preventing fraud.

- **Healthcare**: Improves patient data management, ensuring secure and private access to sensitive records.

- **Voting Systems**: Enables transparent, secure, and immutable voting processes, reducing voter fraud and enhancing democratic processes.

- **Real Estate**: Streamlines property transactions, reducing the need for intermediaries and speeding up processes.

Understanding Decentralized Applications (DApps)

BLOCKCHAIN'S POTENTIAL culminates significantly in Decentralized Applications (DApps), software applications running on a decentralized blockchain network rather than a single centralized server. DApps are characterized by:

- **Open Source**: Transparency in code and operations, publicly accessible for verification.

- **Decentralized**: Operates on peer-to-peer networks without central authorities.

- **Incentivization**: Network participants are often incentivized through tokens or cryptocurrencies.

- **Immutability and Security**: Transactions and records maintained transparently and immutably on the blockchain.

A typical DApp might leverage Ethereum's smart contract capabilities to facilitate decentralized finance (DeFi), gaming, decentralized exchanges (DEXs), or social networking, offering censorship-resistant platforms and democratized governance.

Conclusion

BLOCKCHAIN TECHNOLOGY'S foundational concepts provide the necessary structure for decentralized solutions that challenge traditional centralized models. By understanding its principles—cryptographic security, decentralized governance, immutable transactions, and consensus mechanisms—developers, businesses, and innovators can harness blockchain to drive digital transformation across industries.

As we continue deeper into blockchain and decentralized applications, the following chapters build upon these fundamentals, exploring blockchain architectures, development environments, smart contracts, DApp construction, security considerations, and real-world use cases, ultimately guiding you toward proficiency in blockchain development.

Evolution and Use Cases of Blockchain

BLOCKCHAIN TECHNOLOGY, though popularly associated with cryptocurrencies, has undergone significant evolution since its inception, transforming itself into a versatile solution applicable across numerous sectors. This section will explore the historical evolution of blockchain and present several use cases, highlighting its versatility and potential impact on various industries.

Historical Evolution of Blockchain

Early Beginnings: Bitcoin and the Genesis of Blockchain

THE CONCEPT OF BLOCKCHAIN technology first materialized in 2008 with the release of the Bitcoin whitepaper by the pseudonymous entity Satoshi Nakamoto. Bitcoin introduced blockchain as a solution to the double-spending problem in digital currencies without relying on intermediaries like banks or payment processors. The creation of Bitcoin marked the first practical implementation of a decentralized digital currency secured through cryptographic methods.

The original Bitcoin blockchain provided fundamental innovations:

- **Distributed Ledger**: Transactions recorded across multiple nodes, eliminating central authority control.
- **Proof of Work (PoW)**: Computational consensus mechanism securing the blockchain against malicious attacks.
- **Cryptographic Security**: Immutable records ensured through cryptographic hashing and digital signatures.

Example of a basic Bitcoin-like transaction representation:

```
{
"sender": "1BvBMSEYstWetqTFn5Au4m4GFg7xJaNVN2",
"recipient": "3J98t1WpEZ73CNmQviecrnyiWrnqRhWNLy",
"amount": 0.25,
```

"timestamp": 1624656000,

"signature": "304402204e45e16932b8af514961a1d53..."

}

Second-Generation Blockchain: Ethereum and Smart Contracts

FOLLOWING BITCOIN'S success, blockchain's potential began attracting developers who saw opportunities far beyond digital currencies. Ethereum, proposed by Vitalik Buterin in 2013 and launched in 2015, significantly expanded blockchain capabilities by introducing smart contracts—self-executing agreements written into code, facilitating automation, and decentralized logic beyond financial transactions.

Ethereum provided advancements such as:

- **Programmable Blockchain**: Developers could write custom smart contracts using Solidity, Ethereum's Turing-complete language.

- **Decentralized Applications (DApps)**: Enabled creation of decentralized software, including financial instruments, decentralized exchanges (DEXs), and marketplaces.

Example Solidity smart contract snippet demonstrating basic token transfer functionality:

```
pragma solidity ^0.8.0;

contract SimpleToken {

mapping(address => uint256) public balanceOf;
```

```
constructor(uint256 initialSupply) {

balanceOf[msg.sender] = initialSupply;

}

function transfer(address to, uint256 amount) public returns (bool)
{

require(balanceOf[msg.sender] >= amount, "Insufficient balance");

balanceOf[msg.sender] -= amount;

balanceOf[to] += amount;

return true;

}

}
```

Third-Generation Blockchain: Scalability, Sustainability, and Interoperability

THE THIRD GENERATION of blockchain platforms emerged in response to limitations observed in Ethereum and Bitcoin, particularly scalability, sustainability, and interoperability. Platforms such as Cardano, Solana, Polkadot, and Cosmos exemplify this wave of innovation:

- **Cardano** introduced proof-of-stake (PoS) consensus and rigorous academic peer-reviewed development processes, emphasizing sustainability and security.

- **Solana** focused on high throughput and scalability, utilizing innovations like Proof-of-History (PoH) to significantly increase transaction speeds.

- **Polkadot** and **Cosmos** pursued blockchain interoperability, enabling cross-chain communication and seamless asset transfers across different blockchain networks.

This evolutionary journey highlights blockchain's rapid progress, driven by continuous experimentation and adaptation.

Prominent Use Cases of Blockchain Technology

BLOCKCHAIN'S APPLICATION scope has rapidly expanded beyond cryptocurrencies, influencing diverse industries with its secure, transparent, and decentralized nature. Below, we examine several prominent blockchain use cases demonstrating real-world impact and innovation.

Financial Services and Decentralized Finance (DeFi)

ONE OF BLOCKCHAIN'S earliest and most profound impacts was felt in financial services through Decentralized Finance (DeFi). DeFi platforms leverage smart contracts and blockchain technology to offer financial services without intermediaries such as banks, brokers, or exchanges.

Key DeFi innovations include:

- **Decentralized Exchanges (DEXs)**: Platforms like Uniswap, SushiSwap, and PancakeSwap allow peer-to-peer asset swaps without centralized intermediaries, reducing fees and increasing transparency.

- **Lending and Borrowing Protocols**: Platforms such as Aave and Compound enable users to lend and borrow digital assets without credit checks or traditional banking intermediaries.

- **Stablecoins**: Cryptocurrencies pegged to stable assets (USD, gold), such as USDC and DAI, providing price stability within blockchain-based ecosystems.

Example DeFi lending logic simplified in Solidity:

```
pragma solidity ^0.8.0;

contract SimpleLending {

mapping(address => uint256) public balances;

function deposit() public payable {

balances[msg.sender] += msg.value;

}

function withdraw(uint256 amount) public {

require(balances[msg.sender] >= amount, "Insufficient balance");

balances[msg.sender] -= amount;

payable(msg.sender).transfer(amount);

}

}
```

Non-Fungible Tokens (NFTs) and Digital Assets

NFTS HAVE EMERGED AS another significant blockchain use case, revolutionizing digital ownership. NFTs are unique, indivisible digital assets secured by blockchain technology, widely adopted in digital art, collectibles, virtual land, and gaming.

Notable NFT platforms include:

- **OpenSea**: The largest NFT marketplace allowing creators and collectors to trade digital art, collectibles, and virtual assets.

- **Decentraland**: A virtual world leveraging NFTs for land ownership, avatars, and digital goods, enabling decentralized virtual experiences.

Example ERC-721 token (NFT standard) in Solidity:

```
pragma solidity ^0.8.0;

import "@openzeppelin/contracts/token/ERC721/ERC721.sol";

contract MyNFT is ERC721 {

uint256 private _tokenIdCounter;

constructor() ERC721("MyNFT", "MNFT") {}

function mintNFT(address recipient) public returns (uint256) {

_tokenIdCounter++;

uint256 newTokenId = _tokenIdCounter;

_mint(recipient, newTokenId);
```

```
return newTokenId;
}
}
```

Supply Chain Management and Transparency

BLOCKCHAIN HAS SIGNIFICANTLY enhanced supply chain transparency and efficiency. Organizations utilize blockchain to trace products from origin to consumer, providing immutable records that prevent fraud and improve operational accountability.

Examples include:

- **IBM Food Trust**: Enables real-time tracking of food products, enhancing food safety and reducing contamination risks.
- **VeChain**: Utilizes blockchain for traceability and authenticity verification in luxury goods, automotive parts, pharmaceuticals, and agriculture.

Healthcare and Patient Records Management

BLOCKCHAIN ENHANCES healthcare data security, patient privacy, and interoperability between healthcare providers. Platforms such as MedRec, Guardtime, and Factom provide solutions for secure patient records management, prescription tracking, and streamlined clinical trials data management.

Identity Verification and Management

DECENTRALIZED IDENTITY solutions leverage blockchain technology to enable secure, user-controlled digital identities. Solutions like uPort, Civic, and Microsoft ION empower users with self-sovereign identities, reducing reliance on centralized databases vulnerable to breaches and identity theft.

Voting and Governance

BLOCKCHAIN IS INCREASINGLY employed to ensure transparent and secure voting processes, leveraging immutability and decentralization. Projects like Horizon State, Follow My Vote, and DAO governance frameworks provide secure, transparent, and tamper-proof voting solutions applicable to corporate, community, and government contexts.

Conclusion: Blockchain's Expanding Horizon

BLOCKCHAIN'S EVOLUTION from a cryptographic solution underpinning Bitcoin to a versatile foundational technology demonstrates its transformative potential. Real-world applications across finance, digital assets, supply chains, healthcare, identity, and governance illustrate blockchain's ability to address transparency, security, and decentralization challenges.

As blockchain matures, continued innovation—such as cross-chain interoperability, enhanced scalability via Layer 2 solutions, and integrations with emerging technologies like AI—will further amplify its impact. By understanding blockchain's historical progression and exploring its practical use cases, individuals and organizations can strategically position themselves within this transformative technological landscape.

Centralized vs. Decentralized Systems

IN TODAY'S INCREASINGLY digital and interconnected world, the architecture of technological solutions profoundly impacts efficiency, reliability, trust, and control. Systems typically fall under two broad categories—centralized and decentralized—each with distinct attributes, advantages, and drawbacks. Understanding these differences is crucial for developers, architects, and decision-makers, especially when designing systems for scalability, transparency, security, and user autonomy.

Understanding Centralized Systems

CENTRALIZED SYSTEMS are architectures where a single authority or entity exercises control over resources, data, and decision-making processes. All operations, decisions, and data flow through a single central server or cluster of servers managed by an organization or individual. Traditional banking systems, most web applications, and large-scale corporate data centers represent typical examples of centralized systems.

Characteristics of Centralized Systems

CENTRALIZED SYSTEMS are distinguished by the following primary characteristics:

- **Single Point of Control**: One central authority manages operations, updates, policies, and data management.
- **Hierarchical Management**: Clear hierarchical structure simplifies governance but may create bottlenecks.

- **Dependency and Vulnerability**: Reliance on a single node or cluster, resulting in potential vulnerabilities and systemic risks.

Advantages of Centralized Systems

CENTRALIZED SYSTEMS provide several clear advantages:

- **Simplified Management**: Centralized authority makes it easier to manage updates, security patches, and policies.

- **Efficient Coordination**: Easier to coordinate and control resources, allowing quick decision-making and unified policy enforcement.

- **Cost Efficiency**: Centralization can reduce infrastructure and administrative costs due to streamlined processes and consolidated resources.

- **Easier Monitoring and Regulation**: Regulatory compliance and auditing become straightforward with centralized control of information.

Limitations of Centralized Systems

HOWEVER, CENTRALIZED systems also present inherent limitations and vulnerabilities:

- **Single Point of Failure**: Centralized systems are highly vulnerable to single points of failure—server downtime, network outages, or cyber-attacks can cripple entire operations.

- **Privacy and Security Risks**: Central storage of sensitive data presents a high-value target for hackers or malicious actors.

- **Lack of Transparency**: Centralized systems may lack accountability, leading to potential misuse of data or resources without users' knowledge or consent.

- **Reduced User Autonomy**: Users must trust the central authority with their data and actions, limiting user autonomy and control.

Decentralized Systems: An Alternative Approach

DECENTRALIZED SYSTEMS distribute data, control, and decision-making across multiple independent nodes or participants. Instead of relying on a single entity, decentralized systems disperse authority and governance, allowing multiple actors to collaborate without central coordination. Blockchain technology, peer-to-peer (P2P) networks, decentralized finance (DeFi), and cryptocurrency exchanges exemplify decentralized system architecture.

Characteristics of Decentralized Systems

DECENTRALIZED SYSTEMS exhibit these defining characteristics:

- **Distributed Control**: Authority and data distributed across numerous nodes or participants, each retaining autonomy.

- **Fault Tolerance**: No single node controls the entire system; the failure of a node does not typically disrupt overall system functionality.

- **Enhanced Transparency**: Transactions and interactions are usually public or distributed transparently among network participants, enabling accountability.

- **Greater User Autonomy**: Users retain greater control over their data, identity, and digital assets.

Advantages of Decentralized Systems

THE BENEFITS OF DECENTRALIZATION have become increasingly recognized:

- **Increased Reliability and Resilience**: Decentralized systems are resilient to single points of failure, providing reliability through redundancy.

- **Enhanced Security**: Eliminating central points of attack reduces vulnerabilities and enhances overall system security.

- **Improved Trust**: Decentralized systems foster trust through transparent processes and consensus-driven operations, reducing reliance on potentially biased or untrustworthy intermediaries.

- **Privacy and Data Sovereignty**: Users have direct control over their information, reducing privacy concerns associated with centralized data management.

Disadvantages of Decentralized Systems

DESPITE NUMEROUS ADVANTAGES, decentralization also introduces certain complexities:

- **Complex Coordination**: Consensus among multiple nodes or participants can slow decision-making, introducing inefficiencies.

- **Scalability Challenges**: Distributed consensus mechanisms (e.g., Proof of Work) can limit scalability and throughput, making decentralized systems slower or resource-intensive.

- **Regulatory and Compliance Issues**: Decentralized systems may face regulatory uncertainty, complicating compliance with jurisdictional requirements.

Comparative Analysis of Centralized vs. Decentralized Architectures

TO ILLUSTRATE THE DIFFERENCES clearly, consider the comparison between centralized and decentralized architectures across key dimensions:

1. Data Integrity and Security

CENTRALIZED:

Data is vulnerable due to a single point of attack. A breach in the central repository compromises the entire dataset.

Decentralized:

Data integrity is robust due to cryptographic validation and consensus mechanisms. Data distributed across nodes makes large-scale breaches significantly harder.

2. System Resilience

CENTRALIZED:

System failures often result in total downtime. A failure at the central node affects all dependent operations.

Decentralized:

Highly resilient to failures. Even if multiple nodes fail, the system remains operational, significantly reducing downtime and service interruptions.

2. Speed and Performance

CENTRALIZED:

Usually faster, with immediate decision-making capabilities due to fewer layers of communication. Ideal for applications requiring high throughput and quick response times.

Decentralized:

Slower, particularly in consensus-based networks like blockchain, where every participant verifies transactions. However, newer technologies like Layer 2 solutions (Polygon, Arbitrum) are addressing scalability issues.

3. Cost and Scalability

CENTRALIZED:

Initially cost-effective and straightforward to scale vertically (adding more power/resources to existing servers). However, horizontal scaling can be costly and complex.

Decentralized:

Easier to scale horizontally by adding more nodes. Yet, transaction fees and network complexity can add overhead in certain systems (e.g., Ethereum gas fees).

4. Governance and Control

CENTRALIZED:

Clear governance structure; decisions made quickly and consistently. Ideal for organizations where rapid, centralized decision-making is crucial.

Decentralized:

Governance dispersed across stakeholders, promoting democratic and transparent decision-making. However, reaching consensus among numerous stakeholders can be time-consuming.

4. Privacy and Transparency

CENTRALIZED:

Low transparency; privacy and security depend entirely on the organization controlling the data.

Decentralized:

High transparency; blockchain ledgers typically offer public transaction visibility, though advanced cryptographic techniques (e.g., zero-knowledge proofs) increasingly enhance privacy.

Example Implementation: Data Storage Comparison

TO BETTER ILLUSTRATE these differences, consider an example scenario of data storage:

Centralized Approach (Example with SQL Database):

```
—Example of centralized user registration database schema

CREATE TABLE Users (

UserID INT PRIMARY KEY AUTO_INCREMENT,

Username VARCHAR(255) UNIQUE NOT NULL,

PasswordHash VARCHAR(255) NOT NULL,

Email VARCHAR(255) UNIQUE NOT NULL,

CreatedAt TIMESTAMP DEFAULT CURRENT_TIMESTAMP

);
```

In this scenario, data is stored centrally, creating dependency on one database server. Breaching this database could expose all user information.

Decentralized Approach (Blockchain Smart Contract Example):

```
pragma solidity ^0.8.0;

contract UserRegistry {

struct User {

address walletAddress;

string username;
```

```
}

mapping(address => User) public users;

function registerUser(string memory _username) public {

require(bytes(users[msg.sender].username).length == 0, "User already registered");

users[msg.sender] = User(msg.sender, _username);

}

}
```

This smart contract represents decentralized user registration on blockchain, allowing users to maintain direct ownership and control over their identities without relying on central databases.

The Future Balance: Hybrid Systems

IN REALITY, MANY MODERN solutions combine elements of both centralized and decentralized architectures to leverage the strengths of each. Hybrid solutions emerge, combining the speed and efficiency of centralized systems with the resilience, transparency, and user autonomy of decentralized architectures.

Conclusion

CHOOSING BETWEEN CENTRALIZED and decentralized architectures depends on the goals, context, and specific use cases. Centralized systems offer simplicity, speed, and streamlined management but risk single points of failure and reduced transparency. Decentralized systems excel in resilience, transparency, and empowerment, though they introduce complexity, slower decision-making, and scalability challenges.

As blockchain and decentralization mature, innovations continue to address existing limitations, resulting in hybrid architectures offering optimal solutions for modern technological and economic challenges. Understanding these differences provides developers, businesses, and stakeholders with critical insights necessary for making informed strategic decisions in today's rapidly evolving digital ecosystem.

Importance of DApps in the Modern Digital Economy

DECENTRALIZED APPLICATIONS, commonly known as DApps, have rapidly emerged as vital components within the modern digital economy. Fueled by the growing prominence of blockchain technologies, smart contracts, and decentralization principles, DApps stand poised to redefine how we conceive, develop, and interact with digital services, products, and platforms.

The digital economy today is defined by interconnectedness, automation, transparency, security, and user-driven value creation. DApps effectively address many of the challenges encountered in traditional centralized applications by providing decentralized, transparent, and user-centric solutions. To appreciate the importance of DApps, it's essential to explore the key advantages they bring, their impact across various sectors, and how they significantly contribute to the evolving economic landscape.

Decentralization: Revolutionizing Digital Trust

TRUST HAS LONG BEEN a challenge in traditional centralized digital systems. Users often must trust centralized authorities, such as banks, social media platforms, or marketplaces, to manage their data and facilitate interactions. DApps, by contrast, rely on blockchain's distributed ledger technology, enabling trustless interactions.

With DApps, trust is decentralized and verifiable. Users don't depend on a single authority; rather, they trust the cryptographic proofs and consensus protocols underpinning the blockchain. This shift fundamentally alters the trust dynamic, creating opportunities for greater transparency and accountability, essential for the digital economy's future.

Enhancing User Sovereignty and Data Ownership

IN THE MODERN DIGITAL landscape, data privacy and user control are increasingly critical concerns. Traditional applications store user data in centralized servers, vulnerable to misuse, breaches, or unauthorized access. DApps transform this model by ensuring user data sovereignty. Users retain control over their personal information, deciding how and when it's shared or utilized.

Consider decentralized identity systems like uPort, Civic, or Microsoft ION, which exemplify user sovereignty principles. These systems allow users to control and share their identity data without intermediaries, significantly enhancing privacy and data autonomy.

Transparency and Auditability

TRANSPARENCY HAS BECOME a fundamental expectation in digital services, particularly in finance, healthcare, and governance. DApps offer unprecedented transparency due to their reliance on public blockchain infrastructure. Every transaction, decision, or modification is recorded immutably and transparently on the blockchain, enabling verifiable audit trails accessible to users, stakeholders, and regulatory bodies alike.

This transparency fosters accountability and trust. Decentralized finance (DeFi) applications such as Uniswap, Aave, and Compound leverage blockchain transparency, giving users insight into how transactions, liquidity pools, lending rates, and governance votes function, thereby promoting informed decision-making.

Enhanced Security and Resilience

DAPPS SIGNIFICANTLY enhance system security and resilience. Centralized platforms represent single points of failure vulnerable to cyberattacks, data breaches, or system downtime. DApps, however, distribute operations and data storage across numerous nodes in the blockchain network. This decentralization creates resilience and robust security mechanisms, making large-scale breaches virtually impossible without substantial coordination.

Additionally, the cryptographic nature of blockchain ensures data integrity and secure user transactions. Cryptographic validation, digital signatures, and public-private key infrastructure collectively reinforce the security layer inherent in DApps.

Enabling Economic Inclusivity and Financial Democratization

ONE OF THE TRANSFORMATIVE impacts of DApps is democratization, particularly in financial services. Traditional financial systems exclude significant portions of the global population lacking access to banking or financial infrastructure. DApps offer inclusive alternatives through decentralized finance (DeFi) platforms.

DeFi applications provide access to lending, borrowing, insurance, investing, and savings services without intermediaries or traditional banking infrastructures. Users worldwide can participate with just an internet connection and crypto wallet. This democratization breaks down economic barriers, enabling financial inclusion, and empowerment globally.

For instance, a simplified example of a decentralized lending protocol in Solidity might look like this:

```
pragma solidity ^0.8.0;

contract DecentralizedLending {

mapping(address => uint256) public balances;

function depositFunds() public payable {

balances[msg.sender] += msg.value;

}

function withdrawFunds(uint256 amount) public {

require(balances[msg.sender] >= amount, "Insufficient balance.");

balances[msg.sender] -= amount;

payable(msg.sender).transfer(amount);

}

}
```

This basic example demonstrates the transparent, inclusive nature of DeFi applications, enabling users to deposit and withdraw funds securely without traditional intermediaries.

Impact Across Diverse Industries

DAPPS' DECENTRALIZED and transparent nature enables disruptive innovation across various sectors, significantly impacting how traditional industries operate.

1. Financial Services (DeFi)

DECENTRALIZED FINANCE platforms revolutionize lending, investing, trading, and payments. DApps such as MakerDAO (stablecoin lending), Uniswap (decentralized exchange), and Aave (lending and borrowing) provide financial services transparently, securely, and without intermediaries, challenging traditional banking systems.

2. Healthcare

IN HEALTHCARE, DAPPS provide secure, transparent patient record management. Platforms such as MedRec and Factom leverage blockchain and decentralized applications to offer immutable patient histories, prescription tracking, and interoperable patient data management among healthcare providers.

3. Supply Chain Management

DAPPS HAVE SIGNIFICANTLY enhanced transparency, traceability, and authenticity in global supply chains. Solutions such as VeChain and IBM Food Trust use decentralized applications and blockchain to trace goods' origin, verify authenticity, and provide transparent audit trails for supply chain participants.

4. Gaming and Digital Entertainment

BLOCKCHAIN-BASED GAMING DApps offer unique opportunities for gamers to own digital assets truly, monetize achievements, and engage in decentralized economies within virtual worlds. Games like Axie Infinity, Decentraland, and CryptoKitties pioneered blockchain gaming and NFT-based digital asset ownership.

5. Governance and Voting Systems

DECENTRALIZED VOTING systems and governance DApps bring transparency, security, and trust to democratic processes. Platforms such as Horizon State and Follow My Vote enable secure voting and decision-making without intermediaries or manipulation.

Economic Efficiency and Cost Reduction

DAPPS OFTEN DELIVER significant economic efficiencies by eliminating intermediaries, automating processes through smart contracts, and streamlining transactions. Reducing intermediary fees, processing times, and manual interventions makes decentralized applications economically advantageous over traditional centralized counterparts.

Encouraging Innovation and Competition

THE OPEN-SOURCE NATURE of most DApps fosters collaborative innovation and healthy competition. Developers worldwide contribute to DApp ecosystems, continuously enhancing functionalities, security, and user experience. The decentralized landscape stimulates rapid experimentation, driving technological advancements benefiting users and developers alike.

The Role of Tokenization in Value Creation

DAPPS FREQUENTLY UTILIZE tokenization to drive user engagement, incentivize behaviors, and facilitate decentralized economies. Tokenization allows real-world or digital assets to be represented on blockchain, enabling transparent ownership, trading, and fractionalization of previously illiquid assets.

Platforms utilizing tokens can reward users, creators, validators, and participants transparently, reinforcing ecosystem growth and stability. For example, Basic Attention Token (BAT) incentivizes users, publishers, and advertisers within the Brave browser ecosystem.

Challenges and Opportunities Ahead

DESPITE NUMEROUS ADVANTAGES, DApps face several challenges in scalability, usability, regulatory compliance, and mass adoption. Slow transaction speeds, high fees (in certain networks), and complex user experiences hinder widespread adoption. Yet, emerging innovations such as Layer 2 solutions (Polygon, Arbitrum), simplified wallet interactions, and evolving regulatory frameworks increasingly address these challenges.

Conclusion: The Integral Role of DApps in Shaping the Digital Economy

THE IMPORTANCE OF DECENTRALIZED applications in the modern digital economy cannot be overstated. Through decentralization, enhanced security, transparency, financial inclusion, innovation, and economic efficiency, DApps represent transformative forces shaping tomorrow's digital landscape.

As developers, entrepreneurs, policymakers, and users increasingly embrace decentralization, blockchain, and smart contract technology, DApps stand poised as central elements enabling a more transparent, secure, inclusive, and user-driven digital economy. Understanding their importance empowers stakeholders across all sectors to harness decentralization's benefits effectively and build robust solutions addressing critical challenges in modern society.

Chapter 2: Fundamentals of Blockchain Architecture

Blocks, Transactions, and Consensus Mechanisms

BLOCKCHAIN TECHNOLOGY is a decentralized ledger that records transactions across multiple computers in such a way that recorded entries cannot be altered retroactively. To fully grasp the fundamentals of blockchain architecture, it's essential to delve deeply into the foundational elements: blocks, transactions, and consensus mechanisms. Each of these components plays a pivotal role in maintaining blockchain's integrity, immutability, and security.

Blocks: The Building Blocks of Blockchain

A BLOCKCHAIN, AT ITS core, is essentially a linked list of blocks. Each block acts as a container holding transactional data. To understand the concept clearly, we can break down the anatomy of a typical blockchain block:

- **Block Header**: Contains critical metadata about the block itself, typically including:

  ○ **Timestamp**: When the block was created.

  ○ **Previous Block Hash**: The cryptographic hash of the preceding block, thus ensuring the chain remains immutable and ordered.

  ○ **Nonce**: A number utilized in the mining process to produce a valid hash.

○ **Merkle Root**: A cryptographic hash of all the transactions in the block, enabling efficient verification of the block contents.

● **Transaction Data**: Contains a batch of valid transactions, usually structured as a list. Each transaction within a block holds details like sender and receiver addresses, transaction amounts, and transaction-specific metadata.

Here's a simplified illustration of a block's JSON representation:

```
{
"block_header": {
"timestamp": "2023-03-05T14:48:00.000Z",
"previous_block_hash":
"00000000000000000769cbbdbdc9825b7...",
"nonce": 284528,
"merkle_root": "3ac674216f3e15c761ee1a5e255f067937"
},
"transactions": [
{
"from": "0x123abc...",
"to": "0x456def...",
"amount": 2.5,
"signature": "0xa8d5f7..."
```

```
},
{
"from": "0x789ghi...",
"to": "0xabc123...",
"amount": 0.75,
"signature": "0xf9c2b1..."
}
]
}
```

This structure ensures every block is interconnected, forming a secure and tamper-proof chain.

Transactions: The Core of Blockchain Activity

TRANSACTIONS REPRESENT the core activity within any blockchain network. A transaction typically involves the transfer of digital assets—such as cryptocurrency tokens—from one address to another. Understanding the lifecycle and validation of a transaction is critical:

- **Initiation**: A transaction begins when a user initiates a request, typically through a blockchain wallet, specifying sender, recipient, and amount.

- **Verification and Broadcasting**: Transactions are cryptographically signed by the sender's private key and then broadcast to the blockchain network.

- **Validation**: Nodes in the network independently verify the transaction for validity, ensuring criteria such as sufficient balance and correct signatures are met.

- **Inclusion in Blocks**: Validated transactions are then grouped by miners or validators into blocks, where they await final confirmation through the consensus process.

Consensus Mechanisms: Securing Decentralization and Trust

CONSENSUS MECHANISMS are protocols that blockchain networks employ to achieve agreement among nodes regarding the ledger's state. They provide blockchain with its decentralized trust mechanism. Different blockchain networks implement different consensus algorithms based on their intended use-case, security requirements, and scalability needs. The primary consensus mechanisms include:

Proof of Work (PoW)

POW WAS THE ORIGINAL consensus algorithm introduced by Bitcoin. Miners compete to solve computationally intensive mathematical puzzles, requiring considerable computational power. The miner who solves the puzzle first gets the right to create the next block, receiving rewards in cryptocurrency. PoW inherently prevents fraud through the enormous computational energy required, making blockchain alteration economically and practically infeasible.

A simplified pseudocode for PoW algorithm looks like this:

```
import hashlib

def proof_of_work(previous_hash, transactions, difficulty):
```

```
nonce = 0
while True:
data = f"{previous_hash}{transactions}{nonce}".encode()
hash_result = hashlib.sha256(data).hexdigest()
if hash_result.startswith("0" * difficulty):
return nonce, hash_result
nonce += 1
previous_hash = "0000000abc123..."
transactions = ["tx1", "tx2", "tx3"]
difficulty = 4
nonce, valid_hash = proof_of_work(previous_hash, transactions, difficulty)
print(f"Nonce found: {nonce} with hash {valid_hash}")
```

PoW's drawback is significant energy consumption and limited transaction throughput, which has led to the development of alternative consensus mechanisms.

Proof of Stake (PoS)

POS ALGORITHMS CHOOSE block validators based on their stake (the number of tokens or cryptocurrency they hold) in the network rather than computational power. The concept behind PoS is to make network participants financially responsible for the accuracy of transactions.

The validator is chosen randomly or through a deterministic selection process based on their stake. Validators who behave maliciously risk losing their stake through a process called slashing, thus incentivizing honest behavior.

Delegated Proof of Stake (DPoS)

DPOS IS A VARIANT OF PoS in which network stakeholders vote to delegate their tokens to a smaller number of trusted validators or "delegates." These delegates are responsible for validating transactions and maintaining the blockchain's integrity. DPoS networks achieve high performance and scalability, making them suitable for high-volume transaction environments.

Byzantine Fault Tolerance (BFT)

BFT ALGORITHMS, SUCH as Practical Byzantine Fault Tolerance (PBFT), enable consensus in networks where some nodes might behave maliciously. PBFT involves multiple rounds of voting to reach consensus and can tolerate up to one-third of malicious or faulty nodes without compromising the network.

Comparing Consensus Mechanisms

Feature	Proof of Work	Proof of Stake	Delegated PoS	BFT
Security	Very High	High	Medium-High	High
Scalability	Low	Moderate	High	Moderate
Energy Efficiency	Low	High	Very High	High
Decentralization	Very High	Moderate-High	Moderate	Moderate-High

UNDERSTANDING THESE consensus mechanisms helps developers select the appropriate blockchain architecture for their DApps based on specific requirements such as security, decentralization, scalability, and energy efficiency.

The Significance of Immutability and Security in Blockchain

THE BLOCKCHAIN ARCHITECTURE ensures immutability by linking blocks cryptographically. Once transactions are validated and blocks created, altering them requires recalculating hashes of all subsequent blocks—a computationally infeasible task, especially in PoW systems.

Blockchain security hinges on cryptographic hashing, digital signatures, and consensus algorithms. Cryptographic hashes ensure data integrity, digital signatures authenticate transaction senders, and consensus mechanisms maintain the blockchain's consistency across distributed nodes.

Conclusion

BLOCKS, TRANSACTIONS, and consensus mechanisms form the foundational components of blockchain architecture. Understanding these elements allows developers and architects to design robust, secure, and scalable blockchain systems tailored to diverse use-cases—from financial transactions and decentralized finance (DeFi) to supply chain management and identity verification solutions. The decentralized nature of blockchain, underpinned by these core components, enables new business models, trustless systems, and unprecedented levels of transparency and security in digital ecosystems.

Public vs. Private Blockchains

BLOCKCHAIN TECHNOLOGY, characterized by decentralization, transparency, and immutability, exists primarily in two fundamental forms: **Public Blockchains** and **Private Blockchains**. Understanding the differences between these two models is crucial for developers, businesses, and organizations seeking to leverage blockchain technology. Each type of blockchain has its own distinct characteristics, strengths, weaknesses, use cases, and implications for data security, privacy, and scalability. This section explores these differences comprehensively, enabling informed decision-making regarding blockchain technology deployment.

Characteristics of Public Blockchains

PUBLIC BLOCKCHAINS are permissionless distributed ledger systems accessible by anyone. They are the most common and widely recognized form of blockchain, exemplified by popular networks such as Bitcoin and Ethereum. Public blockchains offer decentralization in its purest form, characterized by the following traits:

1. Permissionless Participation

ANYONE CAN JOIN A PUBLIC blockchain network as a node, validator, miner, or user without seeking approval from a central authority. The openness of public blockchains ensures equal opportunities for participation and verification of transactions.

2. Complete Transparency

TRANSACTIONS ON A PUBLIC blockchain are visible to all participants, ensuring transparency and accountability. All transactional data is publicly accessible and verifiable by anyone.

3. Decentralization and Distributed Control

CONTROL OVER THE NETWORK does not lie with a single entity or a small group of entities but is distributed across many independent nodes. Decisions regarding network changes and updates usually require consensus among network participants.

4. Cryptoeconomic Incentives

PUBLIC BLOCKCHAINS rely heavily on cryptoeconomic incentives, rewarding participants through cryptocurrencies for securing the network (e.g., mining rewards in Bitcoin or staking rewards in Ethereum).

5. Immutability and Security

THE DECENTRALIZED STRUCTURE ensures a high level of immutability. Once validated and included in the blockchain, transactions cannot be altered or deleted without significant computational effort.

Examples and Use Cases of Public Blockchains

PUBLIC BLOCKCHAINS have significantly impacted numerous industries and are commonly employed in applications where transparency, decentralization, and trustless interactions are essential:

- **Cryptocurrencies (Bitcoin, Litecoin)**: Facilitating decentralized peer-to-peer monetary transactions.

- **Decentralized Finance (DeFi)**: Platforms like Uniswap and Aave leverage Ethereum's public blockchain for trustless financial services.

- **Non-Fungible Tokens (NFTs)**: Digital asset marketplaces utilize Ethereum or Solana public blockchains for proving authenticity and ownership.

- **Decentralized Applications (DApps)**: Applications leveraging public blockchains for gaming, social networking, and content creation platforms.

Advantages and Disadvantages of Public Blockchains

PUBLIC BLOCKCHAINS possess numerous benefits, including:

Advantages:

- High transparency and accountability.
- Robust security due to decentralization.
- Resilient to censorship and centralized control.
- Promotes innovation through open-source collaboration.

However, they also face challenges:

Disadvantages:

- Limited scalability and performance issues (e.g., slow transaction processing speed in Ethereum).
- Higher operational costs (e.g., gas fees).
- Privacy concerns, since data is openly accessible.
- Energy-intensive consensus mechanisms like Proof of Work.

Characteristics of Private Blockchains

PRIVATE BLOCKCHAINS differ significantly from public blockchains. They operate under strict access controls and are typically used within single organizations or groups of businesses that collaborate closely. Private blockchains display the following core attributes:

1. Permissioned Participation

ACCESS IS RESTRICTED, with participants requiring explicit approval from a central authority or consortium. This controlled access ensures participants are known, identifiable entities.

2. Limited Transparency

UNLIKE PUBLIC BLOCKCHAINS, private blockchain transactions are generally not publicly visible. Transparency is limited to the authorized participants, who share data according to predefined privacy rules.

3. Centralized Control and Governance

A SINGLE ENTITY OR consortium usually manages governance, including consensus mechanisms, protocol updates, and permission granting, resulting in a more centralized structure.

4. Scalability and Performance

PRIVATE BLOCKCHAINS can offer significantly improved performance compared to public blockchains, with faster transaction speeds and lower operational costs due to fewer nodes and controlled conditions.

5. Privacy and Confidentiality

PRIVATE BLOCKCHAINS provide better privacy and confidentiality since sensitive information is shared only among approved participants, making them ideal for businesses and regulated environments.

Examples and Use Cases of Private Blockchains

PRIVATE BLOCKCHAINS are particularly suited to industries and scenarios where data privacy, compliance, performance, and controlled access are critical:

- **Enterprise Supply Chain Management (Hyperledger Fabric)**: Tracking supply chain transactions securely and privately among collaborating businesses.

- **Healthcare Data Management**: Managing patient records privately and securely within healthcare consortiums.

- **Financial Institutions and Banks**: Facilitating private inter-bank transfers, compliance verification, and auditability within trusted financial networks (e.g., JPMorgan's Quorum).

- **Internal Enterprise Solutions**: Implementing secure, internal data sharing and management solutions within a single organization.

Advantages and Disadvantages of Private Blockchains

THE CONTROLLED ENVIRONMENT of private blockchains offers numerous strengths:

Advantages:

- Enhanced performance and scalability.

- Higher levels of privacy and confidentiality.

- Efficient governance and decision-making processes.

- Compliance-friendly design, suitable for regulated industries.

Yet, private blockchains also exhibit inherent limitations:

Disadvantages:

- Reduced decentralization, leading to greater reliance on central authority.

- Lower resilience against censorship or malicious interference by the governing entity.

- Limited transparency and fewer opportunities for independent verification.

- Reduced openness potentially restricting innovation.

Comparing Public and Private Blockchains: Key Differences

Criteria	Public Blockchain	Private Blockchain
Access Control	Permissionless (open to all)	Permissioned (restricted access)
Transparency	Fully transparent (publicly viewable)	Controlled transparency (limited visibility)
Governance	Decentralized, consensus-based	Centralized authority or consortium
Scalability	Generally limited scalability	Highly scalable and performant
Security Model	Robust, decentralized security	Centralized security model
Privacy	Limited privacy due to openness	High levels of privacy and confidentiality
Use Cases	Cryptocurrency, DeFi, NFTs, public DApps	Enterprise, healthcare, regulated financial

Hybrid Blockchains: Bridging Public and Private Models

INCREASINGLY, THE BLOCKCHAIN ecosystem is moving towards hybrid models combining both public and private blockchain characteristics. Hybrid blockchains offer flexibility by providing controlled access while preserving some decentralization, transparency, and security benefits. This type of blockchain is ideal for complex scenarios where a combination of private data handling and public accountability is required.

Example Scenario: A hybrid blockchain might involve private data management within an enterprise, with selective publishing of proof-of-validity to a public blockchain to achieve transparency and verifiability.

```
// Example pseudocode of a Hybrid Blockchain Transaction

async function hybridBlockchainTransaction(privateData) {

// Submit private transaction to private blockchain network

const privateBlock = await submitPrivateTransaction(privateData);

// Create cryptographic proof of validity

const proof = createProof(privateBlock.hash);

// Publish proof to public blockchain for verification

await publishProofToPublicBlockchain(proof);

return { privateBlock, publicProof: proof};

}
```

Hybrid blockchain solutions such as Hyperledger Besu or Dragonchain integrate these dual functionalities effectively, enabling organizations to leverage blockchain's strengths in privacy-sensitive environments.

Conclusion

BOTH PUBLIC AND PRIVATE blockchain models have unique strengths and weaknesses, making each suited to specific applications. Public blockchains excel in decentralization, transparency, and censorship resistance, ideal for cryptocurrencies and open platforms. In contrast, private blockchains offer better performance, privacy, control, and compliance, making them optimal for enterprise solutions and sensitive use cases.

Choosing between public and private blockchain depends on clearly defined business requirements, regulatory constraints, and privacy considerations. Additionally, hybrid blockchain approaches increasingly offer sophisticated solutions, combining advantages from both models, addressing the limitations of each type individually.

Ultimately, understanding these distinctions and their implications thoroughly equips organizations to select the blockchain architecture best suited for their strategic goals and operational needs.

Smart Contracts: The Foundation of DApps

SMART CONTRACTS ARE self-executing agreements with the terms directly written into code, running autonomously on a blockchain network. They form the foundation upon which decentralized applications (DApps) are built, enabling automation, transparency, and immutability within blockchain ecosystems. To fully appreciate the significance of smart contracts in decentralized application development, it's essential to thoroughly understand their architecture, lifecycle, best practices, advantages, and potential pitfalls.

Understanding Smart Contracts

A SMART CONTRACT IS essentially a programmable agreement stored and executed on a blockchain network. It automatically executes predefined rules or conditions encoded into its logic, eliminating intermediaries and human intervention. Smart contracts run on blockchain platforms such as Ethereum, Binance Smart Chain, Solana, and others.

Key characteristics of smart contracts include:

- **Automated Execution**: Executes automatically when predetermined conditions are met.

- **Self-contained and Autonomous**: No external enforcement or third-party intermediaries are needed.

- **Transparent and Immutable**: Once deployed, the code and its execution records are public and cannot be altered retroactively.

- **Cryptographically Secure**: Utilizes digital signatures and cryptographic functions to ensure the integrity and authenticity of interactions.

Anatomy of a Smart Contract

A TYPICAL SMART CONTRACT consists of three primary components:

- **State Variables**: Store persistent data and represent the contract's state.

- **Functions**: Logic defining behavior and operations of the smart contract.

- **Events**: Notifications emitted during important actions, allowing external applications to respond and track contract state.

Consider the following basic Solidity smart contract representing a simple wallet:

```
pragma solidity ^0.8.0;

contract SimpleWallet {
```

```
address public owner;

mapping(address => uint256) public balances;

event Deposit(address indexed user, uint256 amount);

event Withdrawal(address indexed user, uint256 amount);

constructor() {

owner = msg.sender;

}

modifier onlyOwner() {

require(msg.sender == owner, "Caller is not owner");

_;

}

function deposit() public payable {

balances[msg.sender] += msg.value;

emit Deposit(msg.sender, msg.value);

}

function withdraw(uint256 amount) public {

require(balances[msg.sender] >= amount, "Insufficient funds");

balances[msg.sender] -= amount;

payable(msg.sender).transfer(amount);

emit Withdrawal(msg.sender, amount);
```

```
}
event Withdrawal(address indexed user, uint256 amount);
}
```

Lifecycle of a Smart Contract

THE LIFECYCLE OF A smart contract typically involves five primary phases:

1. Design and Development

THE SMART CONTRACT development lifecycle begins with defining clear requirements and designing contract logic. This phase includes careful consideration of the specific functionality needed, user interactions, state variables, and error handling.

2. Compilation and Testing

BEFORE DEPLOYMENT, smart contracts must be compiled from their source code into bytecode, which is executable by the blockchain virtual machine (e.g., Ethereum Virtual Machine, EVM). Tools like Remix, Truffle, and Hardhat provide development and testing environments, allowing thorough testing and debugging of smart contract functionality.

Testing typically involves unit testing and simulation tests:

```
// Example of a simple test using Hardhat and ethers.js
describe("SimpleWallet", () => {
it("should deposit ether correctly", async function() {
```

```
const SimpleWallet = await
ethers.getContractFactory("SimpleWallet");

const wallet = await SimpleWallet.deploy();

await wallet.deployed();

await wallet.deposit({ value: ethers.utils.parseEther("1") });

const balance = await wallet.balances(await wallet.owner());

expect(balance).to.equal(ethers.utils.parseEther("1"));

});

}
```

3. Deployment and Verification

DEPLOYMENT INVOLVES sending compiled smart contract bytecode to the blockchain network, paying associated fees (gas), and making the contract publicly accessible. Deployed contracts are assigned a unique blockchain address. It's crucial to verify deployment success and the contract's state to ensure correctness.

3. Interaction and Execution

AFTER DEPLOYMENT, USERS interact with smart contracts through external interfaces or decentralized applications. Execution occurs automatically according to the code's logic and state conditions, triggered by transactions sent to the blockchain.

The Lifecycle of Smart Contracts

ONCE DEPLOYED ON THE blockchain, a smart contract undergoes a lifecycle comprising specific phases:

- **Creation**: Contract code is deployed to the blockchain and becomes publicly accessible.

- **Activation**: The contract is activated when conditions specified in its code are met.

- **Interaction and Execution**: Users initiate transactions, invoking functions that execute automatically.

- **Termination or Destruction**: Contracts may include provisions for self-destruction (via the selfdestruct function in Solidity), though this action should be taken cautiously due to potential security and economic implications.

Importance of Smart Contracts in DApp Development

SMART CONTRACTS UNDERPIN decentralized applications by providing the decentralized, trusted logic layer. Through smart contracts, DApps offer:

- **Automated Trust**: Removing third-party intermediaries reduces costs, increases efficiency, and eliminates centralized points of failure or censorship.

- **Secure Data Management**: Contracts manage state and interactions securely on-chain, mitigating trust issues associated with traditional intermediaries.

- **Transparency and Auditability**: Transactions and state changes are transparent, allowing easy auditability.

- **Programmability and Automation**: Complex logic and conditions can be embedded within contracts, automating processes like escrow management, token exchange, lending, and governance.

Common Use Cases and Applications

SMART CONTRACTS HAVE become indispensable across various industries:

- **Decentralized Finance (DeFi)**:

  - Lending and borrowing (e.g., Compound, Aave).

  - Decentralized exchanges (DEX) like Uniswap.

  - Automated market makers (AMMs).

- **NFT and Tokenization**: Marketplaces for digital assets and collectibles.

- **Supply Chain Management**: Ensuring traceability and transparency across the supply chain.

- **Insurance and Claims Automation**: Triggering automatic payouts when predefined conditions are met (e.g., parametric insurance contracts).

- **Voting and Governance**: DAO operations utilizing decentralized voting mechanisms.

Security Considerations and Vulnerabilities

DESPITE THEIR IMMENSE advantages, smart contracts carry inherent risks due to the immutable nature of blockchain:

- **Code Vulnerabilities**: Errors in smart contract code can lead to exploits (e.g., DAO hack, reentrancy attacks).
- **Economic Attacks**: Front-running or price oracle manipulation.
- **Immutable Code**: Errors deployed to the blockchain become permanent, highlighting the need for thorough auditing and testing before deployment.

To mitigate these risks, best practices include:

- Comprehensive security audits from reputable blockchain security companies.
- Rigorous testing using testnets and automated tools like Mythril and Slither.
- Implementing well-tested design patterns and libraries like OpenZeppelin contracts.

Future of Smart Contracts: Innovations and Developments

THE LANDSCAPE OF SMART contract development continues to evolve, driven by innovation and the challenges developers face. Some trends and future developments include:

- **New Smart Contract Languages**: Alternatives to Solidity, such as Vyper, Move (Aptos, Sui), and Rust

(Solana, NEAR), offer improved security, readability, and performance.

- **Layer 2 Scaling Solutions**: Ethereum Layer 2 solutions like Optimism, Arbitrum, and zk-Rollups enhance contract scalability and reduce transaction costs.

- **Integration with Artificial Intelligence**: AI-driven smart contracts and oracles provide dynamic, adaptive contracts that respond intelligently to changing conditions.

- **Cross-Chain Interoperability**: Facilitating multi-chain communication and asset transfers through bridges and interoperability protocols like Polkadot or Cosmos.

Conclusion

SMART CONTRACTS ARE fundamental to the blockchain and decentralized application ecosystem, offering unprecedented transparency, automation, and trust. By enabling programmable agreements executed autonomously and securely, they empower innovative decentralized applications that transform industries from finance to logistics. However, due diligence, security best practices, and ongoing developments in blockchain technology remain essential to realizing the full potential of smart contracts in an increasingly decentralized world.

Cryptographic Principles and Security

CRYPTOGRAPHY IS THE cornerstone of blockchain technology, ensuring data integrity, privacy, and secure communication within decentralized networks. By leveraging robust cryptographic principles, blockchain systems ensure the secure recording of transactions, safeguarding users' assets and identities. This section comprehensively explores cryptographic concepts fundamental to blockchain, including hashing algorithms, digital signatures, asymmetric cryptography, encryption standards, secure key management, and best practices essential for maintaining blockchain security.

Foundations of Cryptography in Blockchain

CRYPTOGRAPHY INVOLVES techniques for secure communication in the presence of adversaries. Blockchain utilizes cryptographic methods extensively to ensure security and data integrity, specifically:

- **Hash Functions**
- **Asymmetric Cryptography (Public-Key Cryptography)**
- **Digital Signatures**
- **Encryption Algorithms**
- **Secure Key Management**

Below, each of these components will be examined in detail.

Hash Functions and Their Importance

HASH FUNCTIONS FORM the backbone of blockchain security, transforming input data of any length into fixed-length outputs (hashes). A strong hash function has the following essential characteristics:

- **Deterministic**: Identical inputs produce identical hashes.
- **Collision Resistance**: Extremely improbable to generate identical hashes from different inputs.
- **Pre-image Resistance**: Computationally infeasible to reverse-engineer original data from the hash.
- **Avalanche Effect**: Slight changes in input drastically change the hash output.

Commonly used hash functions in blockchain include SHA-256, Keccak-256 (Ethereum), and Blake2b.

Example hash generation using SHA-256 in Python:

```
import hashlib

def generate_hash(data):

return hashlib.sha256(data.encode()).hexdigest()

data = "Blockchain Security"

hashed_data = generate_hash(data)

print(f"Hash of '{data}': {hashed_data}")
```

Hash functions maintain blockchain immutability by linking each block with the hash of the preceding block, creating a secure and tamper-resistant chain.

Public-Key (Asymmetric) Cryptography

BLOCKCHAIN RELIES HEAVILY on asymmetric cryptography to secure user transactions. This cryptographic technique utilizes pairs of mathematically related keys: one public and one private.

- **Public Key**: Publicly known and used to receive transactions.
- **Private Key**: Kept secret, used to authorize (sign) transactions.

The key pair ensures transactions are securely authenticated, and digital identities are verifiable without revealing private keys.

Here's a simplified example of generating a key pair using Python's cryptography library:

```
from cryptography.hazmat.primitives.asymmetric import rsa

from cryptography.hazmat.primitives import serialization

private_key = rsa.generate_private_key(

public_exponent=65537,

key_size=2048

)

public_key = private_key.public_key()

# Serialize keys

pem_private = private_key.private_bytes(

encoding=serialization.Encoding.PEM,
```

```
format=serialization.PrivateFormat.PKCS8,
encryption_algorithm=serialization.NoEncryption()
)
pem_public = public_key.public_bytes(
encoding=serialization.Encoding.PEM,
format=serialization.PublicFormat.SubjectPublicKeyInfo
)
print("Private Key:", pem_private.decode())
print("Public Key:", pem_public.decode())
```

The private key is securely stored and should never be shared, while the public key can be openly distributed to enable secure interactions.

Digital Signatures for Transaction Verification

DIGITAL SIGNATURES authenticate transactions, ensuring that only legitimate owners can authorize the movement of assets. They leverage asymmetric cryptography, ensuring:

- **Authentication**: Verification of sender identity.
- **Integrity**: Ensures data is unchanged in transit.
- **Non-repudiation**: Prevents senders from denying transaction origination.

A digital signature involves the following steps:

1. Hash the transaction data.
2. Sign the hashed data with the sender's private key.
3. Verify the signature with the sender's public key.

Example using ECDSA digital signatures in Python:

```
from cryptography.hazmat.primitives import hashes

from cryptography.hazmat.primitives.asymmetric import ec, utils

from cryptography.exceptions import InvalidSignature

private_key = ec.generate_private_key(ec.SECP256K1())

public_key = private_key.public_key()

message = b"Blockchain transaction data"

message_hash = hashlib.sha256(message).digest()

# Signing the message

signature = private_key.sign(

message_hash,

ec.ECDSA(utils.Prehashed(hashes.SHA256()))

)

# Verifying the signature

try:

public_key.verify(

signature,

message_hash,
```

```
ec.ECDSA(utils.Prehashed(hashes.SHA256()))
)
print("Signature verified successfully.")
except InvalidSignature:
print("Invalid signature!")
```

Digital signatures are essential to trustless blockchain interactions, providing cryptographic proof of authenticity and data integrity.

Encryption Algorithms for Confidentiality

ENCRYPTION IN BLOCKCHAIN safeguards sensitive information by converting data into an unreadable format. Common encryption standards include:

- **Symmetric Encryption (AES)**: Uses one shared key for both encryption and decryption.
- **Asymmetric Encryption (RSA, ECC)**: Uses separate keys, offering stronger security through public-private key pairs.

Blockchain often employs asymmetric encryption to share private data securely:

```
# Encrypting and decrypting data with RSA
from cryptography.hazmat.primitives import asymmetric, padding
message = b"Confidential Blockchain Data"
# Encrypt with recipient's public key
```

```
encrypted_message = public_key.encrypt(
message,
asymmetric.padding.OAEP(
mgf=asymmetric.padding.MGF1(algorithm=hashes.SHA256()),
algorithm=hashes.SHA256(),
label=None
)
)
# Decrypt with recipient's private key
original_message = private_key.decrypt(
encrypted_message,
asymmetric.padding.OAEP(
mgf=asymmetric.padding.MGF1(algorithm=hashes.SHA256()),
algorithm=hashes.SHA256(),
label=None
)
)
print("Original message:", original_message.decode())
```

Encryption ensures transaction privacy, especially critical in private blockchain networks.

Secure Key Management Best Practices

SECURE KEY MANAGEMENT is crucial to blockchain security. Loss or compromise of keys can lead to irreversible asset loss or theft. Key management best practices include:

- **Hardware Wallets**: Store private keys offline, protected by secure hardware.
- **Multi-signature wallets**: Require multiple signatures for transactions, enhancing security.
- **Cold Storage**: Offline storage of keys, minimizing hacking risks.
- **Regular Key Rotation**: Periodic updates of cryptographic keys to limit exposure.

Example multi-signature contract snippet (Solidity):

```
pragma solidity ^0.8.0;

contract MultiSigWallet {

address[] public owners;

uint public requiredSignatures;

constructor(address[] memory _owners, uint _requiredSignatures) {

owners = _owners;

requiredSignatures = _requiredSignatures;

}

// Logic for multi-signature transaction approval
```

```
}
```

Common Security Vulnerabilities and Mitigation

COMMON CRYPTOGRAPHIC vulnerabilities in blockchain applications include:

- **Poor Randomness Generation**: Predictable cryptographic keys.
  - **Mitigation**: Use cryptographically secure random generators (e.g., /dev/urandom).
- **Private Key Exposure**: Leaked keys compromise wallet security.
  - **Mitigation**: Strict access controls, hardware wallets, key rotation policies.
- **Weak Hashing Algorithms**: Susceptible to collisions.
  - **Mitigation**: Utilize robust algorithms like SHA-256, Blake2b, Keccak-256.
- **Replay Attacks**: Duplicate transactions maliciously repeated.
  - **Mitigation**: Implement transaction nonce, timestamp validations.

Regulatory and Compliance Considerations

BLOCKCHAIN'S CRYPTOGRAPHIC foundations can lead to regulatory challenges, particularly related to privacy regulations (e.g., GDPR). Strategies include:

- Implementing privacy-preserving cryptographic solutions like Zero-Knowledge Proofs.
- Transparent consent processes for storing sensitive data on-chain.
- Clear documentation and audits verifying compliance with international cryptographic standards.

Conclusion

CRYPTOGRAPHY IS ESSENTIAL to blockchain security, privacy, and trust. Mastery of cryptographic principles, such as hashing, asymmetric cryptography, digital signatures, encryption, and secure key management, ensures robust blockchain applications. However, developers and organizations must remain vigilant, continuously updating practices to adapt to emerging cryptographic standards, regulatory environments, and evolving cybersecurity threats. A deep understanding of cryptography forms the basis for secure, reliable, and scalable blockchain systems.

Chapter 3: Setting Up a Development Environment for DApp Creation

Choosing the Right Blockchain Platform (Ethereum, Solana, Binance Smart Chain, etc.)

BLOCKCHAIN TECHNOLOGY has witnessed explosive growth and widespread adoption, significantly driven by decentralized applications (DApps). To successfully develop a DApp, it's crucial to select a blockchain platform that aligns with your project's requirements, including scalability, security, transaction costs, developer community, and tooling support. This section comprehensively explores popular blockchain platforms, providing detailed guidance to help developers make informed decisions.

Ethereum

ETHEREUM IS WIDELY regarded as the pioneer platform for DApp development. Launched in 2015 by Vitalik Buterin, Ethereum introduced the concept of smart contracts, significantly expanding blockchain technology beyond cryptocurrency transactions.

Advantages of Ethereum:

- **Maturity and Stability**: As the oldest smart-contract platform, Ethereum has robust developer tools, extensive documentation, and a well-established ecosystem.

- **Developer Community**: Ethereum has the largest developer community in the blockchain space, with ample resources, libraries, tutorials, and support forums.

- **Smart Contracts in Solidity**: Ethereum's Solidity language simplifies writing complex smart contracts, offering developers familiar syntax resembling JavaScript and C++.

- **Decentralization and Security**: Ethereum prioritizes decentralization, security, and censorship resistance through its proof-of-stake consensus mechanism (Ethereum 2.0), significantly enhancing scalability.

Challenges of Ethereum:

- **Transaction Costs (Gas Fees)**: Ethereum is known for occasionally high transaction costs, which can deter users or applications with frequent micro-transactions.

- **Scalability Issues**: Despite Ethereum 2.0 upgrades, scaling remains challenging, prompting reliance on Layer 2 solutions like Polygon, Arbitrum, and Optimism for scalable transactions.

Suitable Use-Cases for Ethereum:

- Decentralized finance (DeFi) applications
- Non-fungible token (NFT) marketplaces
- Decentralized autonomous organizations (DAOs)
- Secure asset transfers and token issuance

Example Ethereum Use-Case:

DEVELOPING A DEFI LENDING platform is most naturally aligned with Ethereum, considering existing DeFi protocols (Compound, Aave) and the rich ecosystem that simplifies integration.

Solana

SOLANA EMERGED AS A high-performance blockchain designed to address Ethereum's scalability challenges. Introduced by Anatoly Yakovenko in 2017, Solana utilizes a unique Proof of History (PoH) consensus mechanism.

Advantages of Solana:

- **High Throughput and Speed**: Solana supports over 50,000 transactions per second (TPS) and sub-second transaction finality, significantly improving user experience for real-time applications.

- **Low Transaction Fees**: Solana transactions typically cost a fraction of a cent, making it ideal for consumer-facing applications and micro-transactions.

- **Developer Tools and Ecosystem**: Solana provides robust tooling (Anchor Framework, Solana CLI) and supports popular languages like Rust, C, and C++.

Challenges of Solana:

- **Centralization Concerns**: Some argue that Solana sacrifices decentralization for performance, with fewer validator nodes than Ethereum.

- **Less Mature Ecosystem**: While growing rapidly, Solana's ecosystem remains smaller compared to Ethereum, potentially limiting available libraries and tools.

Suitable Use-Cases for Solana:

- Real-time decentralized games and metaverse applications

- High-frequency trading applications

- Consumer-focused applications requiring high performance and low costs

Example Solana Use-Case:

A DECENTRALIZED MULTIPLAYER game demanding real-time interactions and low latency transactions benefits significantly from Solana's speed and minimal fees.

Binance Smart Chain (BSC)

BINANCE SMART CHAIN is a blockchain platform developed by Binance to provide an efficient alternative to Ethereum, offering compatibility with Ethereum Virtual Machine (EVM) and Solidity.

Advantages of Binance Smart Chain:

- **Ethereum Compatibility**: BSC supports Solidity smart contracts, simplifying the migration of Ethereum DApps with minimal adjustments.

- **Low Transaction Fees**: Significantly cheaper transaction costs than Ethereum, benefiting DeFi applications and NFT marketplaces.

- **Integration with Binance Exchange**: Strong integration with Binance's ecosystem, facilitating easy fiat-to-crypto onboarding for end-users.

Challenges of Binance Smart Chain:

- **Centralization**: BSC operates with a limited number of validators controlled primarily by Binance and related entities, raising concerns around decentralization.

- **Security Concerns**: BSC-based projects have historically faced various security issues, emphasizing the need for rigorous audits and development practices.

Suitable Use-Cases for BSC:

- Decentralized finance (DeFi) with low-cost transactions

- NFT applications requiring frequent asset minting

- Applications benefiting from Binance's massive user base

Example BSC Use-Case:

LAUNCHING A DECENTRALIZED exchange (DEX) or yield farming platform on BSC leverages Binance's existing crypto user base and low fees, making it accessible for retail investors.

Polkadot

POLKADOT, FOUNDED BY Gavin Wood (Ethereum co-founder), is a blockchain interoperability protocol enabling various blockchains to communicate and collaborate.

Advantages of Polkadot:

- **Blockchain Interoperability**: Polkadot allows distinct blockchains (parachains) to communicate seamlessly, fostering a decentralized internet of blockchains.
- **Customization and Flexibility**: Projects can build custom blockchain environments optimized for specific use cases, enabling innovation beyond traditional smart contract platforms.
- **Governance Model**: Polkadot features a sophisticated on-chain governance mechanism, empowering users and developers to participate actively in network decisions.

Challenges of Polkadot:

- **Complexity**: Building parachains or integrating with Polkadot involves significant complexity and technical expertise.

- **Higher Initial Costs**: Acquiring parachain slots through auctions requires substantial initial funding or community support.

Suitable Use-Cases for Polkadot:

- Cross-chain decentralized applications
- Multi-chain DeFi ecosystems
- Specialized blockchain infrastructure (privacy-focused chains, identity verification platforms)

Example Polkadot Use-Case:

CREATING A DECENTRALIZED identity verification service accessible across multiple blockchain platforms aligns perfectly with Polkadot's interoperability strengths.

Factors to Consider When Choosing a Platform

WHEN DECIDING ON THE best blockchain platform for your DApp, consider the following key factors:

- **Scalability and Throughput**: Determine the application's speed and scalability requirements.
- **Transaction Costs**: Evaluate the application's tolerance to transaction fees, especially for microtransactions.
- **Developer Tooling and Language Support**: Consider your team's expertise and available tooling support.

- **Ecosystem and Community**: Platforms with vibrant communities typically provide extensive resources, libraries, and documentation, accelerating development.

- **Security and Decentralization**: Balance performance requirements against the security and decentralization offered by each platform.

Comparative Analysis (Summary Table)

Feature	Ethereum	Solana	Binance Smart Chain	Polkadot
Transactions per second	~30	50,000+	~300	~1,000+
Average Transaction Cost	High	Low	Low	Moderate
Smart Contract Language	Solidity	Rust, C, C++	Solidity (EVM compatible)	Rust, Solidity
Decentralization Level	High	Moderate	Low	High
Community & Ecosystem	Mature	Growing	Strong (duc to Binance)	Emcrging rapidly
Scalability Solutions	Layer 2	Native	Built-in scalability	Parachains

Final Recommendations

- **Ethereum**: Optimal for robust, secure, and mature DeFi and NFT applications, prioritizing decentralization.

- **Solana**: Ideal for high-performance, real-time applications, gaming, and consumer apps with low transaction costs.

- **Binance Smart Chain**: Best suited for DApps aiming at retail investors, requiring EVM compatibility and low fees.

- **Polkadot**: Recommended for innovative, complex, cross-chain interoperable solutions.

ULTIMATELY, SELECTING the appropriate blockchain platform is foundational for successfully deploying a decentralized application. Developers must weigh each platform's strengths, limitations, and the intended use case to ensure long-term project viability and user satisfaction.

Installing and Configuring Development Tools (Truffle, Hardhat, Remix, etc.)

SUCCESSFULLY DEVELOPING decentralized applications (DApps) requires specialized development tools designed explicitly for blockchain environments. These tools streamline common tasks such as creating, compiling, testing, debugging, and deploying smart contracts. This section explores the installation, configuration, and usage of the most widely used blockchain development tools: **Truffle**, **Hardhat**, and **Remix**.

Truffle Framework

TRUFFLE IS ONE OF THE most popular Ethereum-based blockchain development frameworks. It provides a comprehensive suite of tools for building, deploying, and testing smart contracts.

Installing Truffle

ENSURE YOU HAVE NODE.js installed first. If not, download it fromnodejs.org[1]:

Check Node.js installation

node -v

npm -v

Install Truffle globally via npm

npm install -g truffle

Verify installation

truffle version

Creating a New Project with Truffle

TO CREATE A NEW TRUFFLE project, follow these steps:

Create a new project directory

mkdir MyDApp

cd MyDApp

Initialize Truffle

truffle init

Your project structure will look like this:

MyDApp/

1. https://nodejs.org

```
├── contracts/
│   └── Migrations.sol
├── migrations/
│   └── 1_initial_migration.js
├── test/
├── truffle-config.js
└── package.json
```

Configuring Truffle

THE PRIMARY CONFIGURATION for Truffle projects is handled through the truffle-config.js file. A typical configuration includes compiler settings, network configurations, and deployment strategies:

```
module.exports = {
networks: {
development: {
host: "127.0.0.1",
port: 8545,
network_id: "*"
},
ropsten: {
```

```
provider: () => new HDWalletProvider(MNEMONIC,
`https://ropsten.infura.io/v3/${INFURA_KEY}`),
network_id: 3,
gas: 5500000,
confirmations: 2,
timeoutBlocks: 200,
skipDryRun: true
}
},
compilers: {
solc: {
version: "^0.8.0",
settings: {
optimizer: {
enabled: true,
runs: 200
}
}
}
}
};
```

Install @truffle/hdwallet-provider to interact with remote Ethereum nodes securely:

```
npm install @truffle/hdwallet-provider dotenv
```

Create a .env file for sensitive data:

```
INFURA_KEY=your-infura-api-key

MNEMONIC=your-wallet-mnemonic
```

Include environment variables securely in your configuration:

```
require('dotenv').config();

const HDWalletProvider = require('@truffle/hdwallet-provider');

const { MNEMONIC, INFURA_KEY } = process.env;
```

Compiling Smart Contracts with Truffle

USE THE FOLLOWING COMMAND to compile smart contracts:

```
truffle compile
```

The compiled contracts appear in the /build folder as JSON artifacts.

Deploying Smart Contracts with Truffle

DEPLOYMENT IS HANDLED through migration scripts placed within the migrations directory:

Example migration script (2_deploy_contracts.js):

```
const MyContract = artifacts.require("MyContract");
```

```
module.exports = function(deployer) {

deployer.deploy(MyContract);

};
```

Deploy to a network using:

```
truffle migrate—network development
```

Hardhat Development Environment

HARDHAT IS A POWERFUL Ethereum development environment favored for its flexibility, speed, and strong developer experience.

Installing Hardhat

INSTALL HARDHAT IN your project's root directory:

```
npm init -y

npm install—save-dev hardhat
```

Initialize a Hardhat project:

```
npx hardhat
```

Follow the interactive prompts, and select "Create a basic sample project."

Your directory structure will resemble:

```
MyHardhatProject/

├── contracts/

│ └── MyContract.sol
```

```
├── scripts/
│   └── deploy.js
├── test/
│   └── MyContract.js
├── hardhat.config.js
└── package.json
```

Configuring Hardhat

EDIT THE HARDHAT.CONFIG.js file for customized network configurations:

```
require("@nomiclabs/hardhat-waffle");
require("dotenv").config();
module.exports = {
solidity: "0.8.4",
networks: {
hardhat: {},
rinkeby: {
url: `https://rinkeby.infura.io/v3/${process.env.INFURA_KEY}`,
accounts: [process.env.PRIVATE_KEY]
}
}
```

};

Install dependencies required for deployment and testing:

npm install—save-dev @nomiclabs/hardhat-waffle ethereum-waffle chai ethers @nomiclabs/hardhat-ethers dotenv

Writing and Deploying Contracts with Hardhat

DEPLOYMENT SCRIPT EXAMPLE (scripts/deploy.js):

async function main() {

const [deployer] = await ethers.getSigners();

console.log("Deploying contracts with the account:", deployer.address);

const MyContract = await ethers.getContractFactory("MyContract");

const myContract = await MyContract.deploy();

console.log("MyContract deployed to:", myContract.address);

}

main().catch((error) => {

console.error(error);

process.exitCode = 1;

});

Run this deployment script:

npx hardhat run scripts/deploy.js—network rinkeby

Testing with Hardhat

TESTING SMART CONTRACTS is straightforward using Hardhat and Mocha:

Example (test/MyContract.js):

```
describe("MyContract", function () {

it("Should deploy and verify initial value", async function () {

const MyContract = await ethers.getContractFactory("MyContract");

const contract = await MyContract.deploy();

await contract.deployed();

expect(await contract.value()).to.equal(42);

});

});
```

Run tests with:

```
npx hardhat test
```

Remix IDE

REMIX IS A BROWSER-based Integrated Development Environment (IDE) ideal for quickly prototyping and deploying smart contracts.

Using Remix IDE

VISIT REMIX.ETHEREUM.org to start immediately.

Creating and Compiling Smart Contracts

- Create a new file (MyContract.sol) in the workspace.
- Write Solidity contracts directly in the browser.
- Remix automatically compiles contracts, displaying errors and warnings.

Deploying Contracts via Remix

- Select deployment environment (JavaScript VM, Injected Web3 via MetaMask, or Web3 Provider).
- Click "Deploy" to deploy the contract.

REMIX PROVIDES AN INTUITIVE interface for interacting with deployed contracts directly from the browser.

Remix for Testing and Debugging

REMIX INCLUDES POWERFUL debugging features:

- Solidity debugger integrated directly in-browser.
- Transaction tracing with visual breakdowns of gas usage and function calls.
- Solidity unit tests using Remix Test Framework.

Example unit test using Remix:

```
pragma solidity ^0.8.0;

import "remix_tests.sol";
```

```
import "../contracts/MyContract.sol";

contract MyContractTest {

MyContract myContract;

function beforeEach() public {

myContract = new MyContract();

}

function testInitialValue() public {

Assert.equal(myContract.value(), 42, "Initial value should be 42");

}

}
```

Run tests directly within Remix using the testing plugin.

Comparing Tools

Feature	Truffle	Hardhat	Remix IDE
Environment	Node.js CLI	Node.js CLI	Browser-based IDE
Project Initialization	Simple	Interactive	Instant
Testing Support	Mocha, Chai	Mocha, Chai	Built-in framework
Deployment Flexibility	High	Very High	Moderate
Debugging	CLI-based	CLI-based (advanced)	Visual, integrated
Solidity Compiler	Customizable	Highly Customizable	Auto (built-in)

BY CAREFULLY INSTALLING, configuring, and mastering these foundational blockchain development tools—Truffle, Hardhat, and Remix—you establish a powerful workflow that significantly enhances your productivity, code quality, and deployment efficiency when building decentralized applications.

Setting Up a Local Blockchain (Ganache, Testnets)

A CRUCIAL STEP IN DECENTRALIZED application (DApp) development is setting up a reliable local blockchain environment. This facilitates rapid development, debugging, testing, and experimentation without incurring transaction fees or delays associated with public blockchain networks. Two primary methods for achieving this are through local blockchain instances such as

Ganache, and public Ethereum test networks (testnets) like Rinkeby, Ropsten, Goerli, and Sepolia.

Local Blockchain with Ganache

GANACHE, PART OF THE Truffle Suite, is one of the most widely used local blockchain emulators, providing developers with a complete Ethereum blockchain experience on their local machine. Ganache simplifies blockchain development by offering immediate block mining, accounts preloaded with Ether, transaction logging, and detailed debugging information.

Installing Ganache

GANACHE IS AVAILABLE in two forms:

- **Ganache CLI**: Command-line interface for advanced developers.
- **Ganache GUI**: A user-friendly graphical interface.

To install Ganache CLI:

npm install -g ganache-cli

To verify the installation:

ganache-cli—version

For Ganache GUI, download and install directly from Truffle's official Ganache page.

Running Ganache CLI

TO START A LOCAL BLOCKCHAIN quickly, simply run:

ganache-cli

By default, Ganache starts a blockchain at http://127.0.0.1:8545, providing 10 Ethereum accounts with 100 ETH each. You'll see output similar to:

Ganache CLI v6.12.2 (ganache-core: 2.13.2)

Available Accounts

==================

(0) 0x1a2b...cdef (100 ETH)

(1) 0x3f4d...abcd (100 ETH)

...

Private Keys

==================

(0) 0xabc123...

(1) 0xdef456...

Listening on 127.0.0.1:8545

Integrating Ganache with Development Tools (Truffle/ Hardhat)

CONFIGURE YOUR TRUFFLE project (truffle-config.js) to connect with Ganache:

module.exports = {

networks: {

```
development: {
host: "127.0.0.1",
port: 8545,
network_id: "*" // Match any network id
}
}
};
```

Then, deploy your contracts using:

```
truffle migrate—network development
```

With Hardhat (hardhat.config.js):

```
module.exports = {
networks: {
localhost: {
url: "http://127.0.0.1:8545"
}
},
solidity: "0.8.4"
};
```

Deploy contracts using Hardhat scripts:

```
npx hardhat run scripts/deploy.js—network localhost
```

Advanced Ganache Configuration

GANACHE CLI ALLOWS customized setups for specific use-cases:

- **Specify accounts and Ether balances:**

ganache-cli—accounts=20—defaultBalanceEther=500

- **Set deterministic mnemonic (useful for reproducible environments):**

ganache-cli -m "candy maple cake sugar pudding cream honey rich smooth crumble sweet treat"

- **Forking Ethereum Mainnet (for testing against real data):**

ganache-cli—fork https://mainnet.infura.io/v3/<INFURA_KEY>

Using Public Testnets

WHILE LOCAL BLOCKCHAINS are ideal for rapid iteration and initial testing, developers eventually need a test environment that closely resembles the production blockchain. Ethereum's public testnets such as Ropsten, Rinkeby, Goerli, and Sepolia provide realistic conditions to validate your application's performance, security, and compatibility.

Choosing a Testnet

EACH ETHEREUM TESTNET has unique characteristics:

- **Ropsten (deprecated)**: Previously popular due to its similarity to Ethereum Mainnet, using proof-of-work consensus. (Officially deprecated.)

- **Rinkeby (deprecated)**: Uses proof-of-authority consensus and is supported by multiple faucets. (Officially deprecated.)

- **Goerli**: Actively maintained; recommended for reliable testing with proof-of-stake consensus.

- **Sepolia**: The recommended testnet moving forward, designed for developers with stable performance and minimal congestion.

It's currently recommended to use **Goerli or Sepolia** for all new DApp developments.

Obtaining Testnet ETH

TO TEST YOUR DAPPS on a public testnet, you'll need testnet ETH. Obtain ETH from faucets:

- Goerli Faucet:https://goerlifaucet.com[2]

- Sepolia Faucet:https://sepoliafaucet.com[3]

Configuring Development Tools for Testnets

USING TRUFFLE (TRUFFLE-config.js):

const HDWalletProvider = require('@truffle/hdwallet-provider');

2. https://goerlifaucet.com/

3. https://sepoliafaucet.com/

```
require('dotenv').config();

module.exports = {

networks: {

goerli: {

provider: () => new HDWalletProvider(process.env.MNEMONIC, `https://goerli.infura.io/v3/${process.env.INFURA_KEY}`),

network_id: 5,

confirmations: 2,

timeoutBlocks: 200,

skipDryRun: true

}

},

compilers: {

solc: {

version: "^0.8.0"

}

}

};
```

Using Hardhat (hardhat.config.js):

```
require("@nomiclabs/hardhat-waffle");
```

```
require("dotenv").config();
module.exports = {
solidity: "0.8.4",
networks: {
goerli: {
url: `https://goerli.infura.io/v3/${process.env.INFURA_KEY}`,
accounts: [process.env.PRIVATE_KEY]
}
}
};
```

Deploy contracts using:

```
truffle migrate—network goerli
```

Or with Hardhat:

```
npx hardhat run scripts/deploy.js—network goerli
```

Monitoring and Debugging Transactions on Testnets

AFTER DEPLOYING CONTRACTS, monitor them via blockchain explorers:

- **Goerli**: https://goerli.etherscan.io
- **Sepolia**: https://sepolia.etherscan.io

Debugging Common Issues

IF YOUR TRANSACTIONS fail on testnets, common troubleshooting steps include:

- Confirming your wallet has sufficient test ETH.
- Ensuring network RPC endpoints (like Infura, Alchemy) are correctly configured.
- Verifying contract compilation settings match the testnet requirements.

Automating Testing with Local Blockchains

USING GANACHE, AUTOMATE testing and continuous integration (CI):

Example automated testing with Mocha/Chai:

```
const MyContract = artifacts.require("MyContract");

contract("MyContract Test Suite", accounts => {

it("should correctly initialize", async () => {

const instance = await MyContract.deployed();

const value = await instance.value();

assert.equal(value, 42, "Initial value should be 42");

});

});
```

Run your tests with Ganache in the background:

```
ganache-cli &

truffle test
```

For automated CI, integrate GitHub Actions with Ganache CLI to run comprehensive test suites automatically on each commit.

Best Practices When Using Local Blockchains and Testnets

- **Always test locally first**: Develop and debug locally before deploying to testnets.
- **Secure your mnemonic and private keys**: Never share private keys publicly or commit them to version control. Use .env files and .gitignore to manage sensitive data securely.
- **Automate contract verification**: Use automated scripts to verify smart contracts on Etherscan after deployment for transparent community interactions.

SETTING UP AND MASTERING local blockchain environments like Ganache, combined with leveraging Ethereum testnets, ensures robust and secure smart contract development. These best practices streamline workflows, minimize costs, enhance security, and significantly accelerate the DApp development lifecycle, preparing your projects effectively for eventual Mainnet deployment.

Writing and Deploying Smart Contracts

SMART CONTRACTS SERVE as the foundational building blocks of decentralized applications (DApps). These autonomous, self-executing contracts enforce rules directly on the blockchain, automating transactions and interactions without intermediaries. Writing secure, efficient smart contracts, followed by reliable deployment processes, is essential to successful blockchain application development. This section comprehensively guides you through the process of creating, testing, and deploying smart contracts, primarily using Solidity and popular tools such as Truffle, Hardhat, and Remix.

Understanding Smart Contract Basics

BEFORE DIVING INTO the specifics of writing and deploying smart contracts, it's essential to understand their fundamental characteristics:

- **Immutable**: Once deployed, the code of smart contracts cannot be altered.
- **Transparent**: Contract code and transactions are visible publicly on the blockchain.
- **Autonomous Execution**: Contracts execute automatically based on predefined logic and triggers.

These traits highlight why rigorous development and testing practices are critical for successful smart contract implementation.

Writing Smart Contracts with Solidity

SOLIDITY REMAINS THE most widely adopted language for developing Ethereum-based smart contracts. It's a statically typed, object-oriented language designed specifically for blockchain environments, resembling syntax from languages like JavaScript and C++.

Creating a Basic Smart Contract

HERE'S AN EXAMPLE OF a simple Solidity contract representing a basic cryptocurrency token (ERC-20 simplified version):

```
// SPDX-License-Identifier: MIT

pragma solidity ^0.8.0;

contract SimpleToken {

string public name = "My Token";

string public symbol = "MTK";

uint256 public totalSupply = 1000000;

mapping(address => uint256) public balanceOf;

event Transfer(address indexed from, address indexed to, uint256 value);

constructor() {

balanceOf[msg.sender] = totalSupply;

}
```

```
function transfer(address _to, uint256 _value) public returns (bool success) {
require(balanceOf[msg.sender] >= _value, "Insufficient balance");
balanceOf[msg.sender] -= _value;
balanceOf[_to] += _value;
emit Transfer(msg.sender, _to, _value);
return true;
}
}
```

Key Solidity Concepts Illustrated Above:

- **State Variables**: Persistently stored data (name, symbol, totalSupply).
- **Mappings**: Data structures for key-value pairs (balanceOf mapping).
- **Events**: Logs blockchain transactions (Transfer event).
- **Constructor**: Initializes the contract state upon deployment.
- **Functions**: Allow interactions and transactions (transfer function).

Compiling Smart Contracts

BEFORE DEPLOYING, SMART contracts must be compiled to bytecode understandable by Ethereum Virtual Machine (EVM). Both Truffle and Hardhat simplify compilation through CLI commands.

Compiling with Truffle:

RUN THE FOLLOWING COMMAND in your Truffle project directory:

truffle compile

Truffle will generate compiled contract artifacts stored in the build/ contracts/ directory.

Compiling with Hardhat:

USE THE FOLLOWING COMMAND within a Hardhat project directory:

npx hardhat compile

Hardhat generates contract artifacts in the artifacts/ directory.

Writing Deployment Scripts

ONCE YOUR SMART CONTRACTS compile successfully, create deployment scripts for deployment to local blockchains or test networks.

Truffle Deployment Example (migrations/2_deploy_token.js):

```
CONST SIMPLETOKEN = artifacts.require("SimpleToken");

module.exports = function(deployer) {

deployer.deploy(SimpleToken);

};
```

Hardhat Deployment Example (scripts/deploy.js):

```
ASYNC FUNCTION MAIN() {

const [deployer] = await ethers.getSigners();

console.log("Deploying contract with the account:", deployer.address);

const Token = await ethers.getContractFactory("SimpleToken");

const token = await Token.deploy();

await token.deployed();

console.log("SimpleToken deployed to:", token.address);

}

main().catch((error) => {

console.error(error);

process.exitCode = 1;

});
```

Deploying Smart Contracts

WITH DEPLOYMENT SCRIPTS in place, deploy your contract to either a local blockchain (e.g., Ganache) or a testnet (e.g., Goerli).

Deploying Locally with Truffle:

TRUFFLE MIGRATE—NETWORK development

Deploying to Testnet with Truffle (Goerli):

TRUFFLE MIGRATE—NETWORK goerli

Deploying Locally with Hardhat:

ENSURE A LOCAL BLOCKCHAIN is running (Ganache or Hardhat node):

npx hardhat node

Deploy your contract to the local network:

npx hardhat run scripts/deploy.js—network localhost

Deploying to Testnet with Hardhat (Goerli):

NPX HARDHAT RUN SCRIPTS/deploy.js—network goerli

Verifying Smart Contract Deployment

AFTER DEPLOYING YOUR contract, verify the deployment status and interactions using block explorers.

- **For local networks (Ganache)**: Monitor logs directly in your CLI.
- **For Ethereum testnets (Goerli)**: Use Etherscan.

Verifying Contracts on Etherscan (Hardhat Example):

FIRST, INSTALL THE Hardhat Etherscan plugin:

```
npm install @nomiclabs/hardhat-etherscan
```

Update hardhat.config.js:

```
require("@nomiclabs/hardhat-etherscan");

require('dotenv').config();

module.exports = {

solidity: "0.8.4",

networks: {

goerli: {

url: `https://goerli.infura.io/v3/${process.env.INFURA_KEY}`,

accounts: [process.env.PRIVATE_KEY]

}

},

etherscan: {

apiKey: process.env.ETHERSCAN_API_KEY

}
```

};

Then verify the contract using:

npx hardhat verify—network goerli DEPLOYED_CONTRACT_ADDRESS

Best Practices for Secure Deployment

DEPLOYING SMART CONTRACTS securely requires attention to crucial security aspects:

- **Use Separate Wallets for Deployment**: Maintain deployment wallets separately from your primary wallets.
- **Secure Private Keys**: Use .env files and environment variables; never commit private keys to public repositories.
- **Audit and Test Thoroughly**: Conduct unit tests, integration tests, and consider professional security audits before Mainnet deployments.

Automating Deployment Pipelines

AUTOMATED CONTINUOUS integration and deployment (CI/CD) pipelines significantly streamline deployment workflows. Popular automation tools include GitHub Actions, CircleCI, and Jenkins.

GitHub Actions Workflow Example (Hardhat):

CREATE A .GITHUB/WORKFLOWS/deploy.yml file:

```
name: Deploy to Goerli
on:
push:
branches:
- main
jobs:
deploy:
runs-on: ubuntu-latest
steps:
- uses: actions/checkout@v3
- uses: actions/setup-node@v3
with:
node-version: '18'
- name: Install dependencies
run: npm install
- name: Compile Contracts
run: npx hardhat compile
- name: Deploy Contracts
env:
PRIVATE_KEY: ${{ secrets.PRIVATE_KEY }}
```

INFURA_KEY: ${{ secrets.INFURA_KEY }}

run: npx hardhat run scripts/deploy.js—network goerli

This automation ensures deployments occur securely and consistently on each push to the primary branch.

Monitoring and Upgrading Smart Contracts

ONCE DEPLOYED, MONITORING smart contracts for performance and security is essential. Tools like Tenderly, Blocknative, and Etherscan provide transaction tracing and real-time monitoring.

Smart contracts are immutable by nature. However, developers may implement patterns like proxy contracts (Upgradeable Contracts pattern) allowing contract logic upgrades without changing the contract address.

By carefully following this structured approach—writing clean, efficient Solidity contracts, rigorously compiling and testing, thoughtfully deploying, securely verifying, and continuously monitoring—you establish a robust foundation for developing reliable decentralized applications.

Chapter 4: Mastering Smart Contract Development

Introduction to Solidity Programming

SOLIDITY IS A HIGH-level, statically-typed programming language specifically designed for developing smart contracts on Ethereum and Ethereum-compatible blockchain platforms. Created by Gavin Wood and Christian Reitwiessner, Solidity enables developers to write secure, transparent, and immutable code that runs exactly as programmed without the possibility of downtime, censorship, or third-party interference.

In this section, we'll deeply explore Solidity, examining its core concepts, syntax, data structures, control flow statements, functions, and best practices. By the end of this section, you'll gain a solid understanding of Solidity and be equipped to start developing robust, secure smart contracts.

Solidity Programming Environment

TO WRITE AND COMPILE Solidity code, developers typically use specialized IDEs (Integrated Development Environments) and browser-based editors. Commonly used tools include:

- **Remix IDE**: A powerful, browser-based IDE that allows you to write, debug, compile, and deploy smart contracts directly from your browser.

- **Visual Studio Code**: A widely popular code editor with a dedicated Solidity extension, providing syntax highlighting, linting, and compilation support.

- **Truffle and Hardhat**: Development frameworks with built-in Solidity compilers that facilitate streamlined deployment, testing, and debugging.

A basic Solidity file has the extension .sol. Here's a simple template for a Solidity file structure:

```
// SPDX-License-Identifier: MIT

pragma solidity ^0.8.0;

contract HelloWorld {

string public message;

constructor(string memory initMessage) {

message = initMessage;

}

function updateMessage(string memory newMessage) public {

message = newMessage;

}

}
```

Let's briefly analyze this snippet:

- **pragma solidity ^0.8.0;** specifies the compiler version used.
- **contract** is the keyword defining a new smart contract.
- **constructor** is a special function executed once during contract deployment.

- **public** variables automatically generate getter functions.

Solidity Syntax and Key Features

SOLIDITY SHARES SIMILARITIES with JavaScript and C++, making it approachable for developers familiar with those languages. The following are essential aspects of Solidity syntax:

Comments

COMMENTS ARE ANNOTATIONS to make code readable and understandable:

Single-line comments:

solidity

// This is a single-line comment

-

Multi-line comments:

solidity

/*

This is a multi-line comment.

Useful for longer explanations.

*/

-

Variables and Data Types

SOLIDITY IS STATICALLY typed, meaning each variable has a fixed type defined explicitly. Some core data types include:

- **Integer**: uint (unsigned), int (signed), e.g., uint256 balance;
- **Boolean**: bool, e.g., bool isActive = true;
- **Address**: address, holds Ethereum addresses, e.g., address payable owner;
- **String**: For text data, e.g., string memory greeting = "Hello";
- **Bytes**: Fixed-size (bytes32) or dynamic (bytes) raw data

Example usage:

uint256 public count = 0;

bool public isValid = false;

address public contractOwner;

Control Flow Statements

SOLIDITY PROVIDES FAMILIAR conditional and looping constructs:

If/Else Conditionals:

solidity

if (balance > 100 ether) {

```
// execute this block
} else {
// alternative execution
}
```

-

Loops:

```solidity
for (uint i = 0; i < 10; i++) {
// loop body
}
uint counter = 0;
while (counter < 5) {
counter++;
}
```

-

Functions in Solidity

FUNCTIONS DEFINE THE actions or interactions within a contract:

- **Visibility Specifiers:**
  - public: accessible externally and internally.

- private: accessible only internally.
- external: only callable externally.
- internal: callable within the contract and derived contracts.

Example function declaration:

```
function transferFunds(address payable recipient, uint256 amount) public returns (bool) {

recipient.transfer(amount);

return true;

}
```

Function Modifiers

MODIFIERS ARE REUSABLE code blocks that control function behavior. Commonly used for access control:

```
modifier onlyOwner {

require(msg.sender == owner, "Not authorized");

_;

}

function withdraw(uint256 amount) public onlyOwner {

payable(owner).transfer(amount);

}
```

Solidity Advanced Features

Events and Logging

EVENTS ENABLE CONTRACT logging, providing transparency to users:

```
event FundTransferred(address indexed from, address indexed to, uint256 amount);

function sendFunds(address payable receiver, uint256 value) public {

receiver.transfer(value);

emit FundTransferred(msg.sender, receiver, value);

}
```

Structs and Arrays

STRUCTS ALLOW GROUPING related variables together. Arrays store collections:

```
struct User {

address userAddress;

uint256 balance;

}

User[] public users;

function addUser(address newUser) public {

users.push(User(newUser, 0));
```

```
}
```

Mappings

MAPPINGS STORE KEY-value pairs efficiently:

```
mapping(address => uint256) public balances;

function updateBalance(address user, uint256 newBalance) public {

balances[user] = newBalance;

}
```

Solidity Error Handling and Exception Management

ERROR HANDLING IN SOLIDITY is crucial for security:

require: Validates conditions before execution.

solidity

```
require(balance > amount, "Insufficient balance");
```

-

assert: Checks invariants (internal consistency).

solidity

```
assert(totalSupply == circulatingSupply + lockedTokens);
```

-

revert: Explicitly reverts transactions.

solidity

```
if (withdrawAmount > balance) {

revert("Withdrawal exceeds balance");

}
```

•

Best Practices in Solidity Programming

ADHERING TO BEST PRACTICES ensures robust, secure smart contracts:

- **Code Readability**: Clearly comment and structure your code.
- **Gas Optimization**: Minimize gas usage by optimizing loops, avoiding unnecessary storage access, and efficient data packing.
- **Security Checks**: Always implement input validation and access control.
- **Avoid External Calls in Loops**: Prevent risks related to external contract calls within loops.
- **Use Libraries for Reusable Code**: Improve code maintainability and readability by leveraging Solidity libraries.

Solidity Development Workflow

TO CREATE SECURE, ROBUST smart contracts, follow these standard steps:

1. **Design**: Clearly outline requirements, functionality, and

use cases.

2. **Implementation**: Write structured and optimized Solidity code.
3. **Compilation and Testing**: Compile and thoroughly test using frameworks like Truffle, Hardhat, or Remix.
4. **Deployment**: Deploy initially to testnets (Ropsten, Goerli, Sepolia) for thorough testing.
5. **Security Audits**: Conduct code audits and vulnerability checks.
6. **Mainnet Deployment**: Deploy carefully on Ethereum Mainnet or compatible chains.

Resources for Solidity Development

CONTINUED LEARNING and reference materials:

- Solidity Documentation
- Remix IDE
- Truffle Suite[4]
- OpenZeppelin Libraries

This introduction to Solidity programming provides a foundational understanding and prepares you for practical smart contract development, which we'll explore in greater depth throughout the rest of this chapter.

Writing, Compiling, and Deploying Smart Contracts

ONCE FAMILIAR WITH Solidity basics, the next crucial step in DApp development is writing, compiling, and deploying smart

4. https://trufflesuite.com/

contracts effectively. This section will guide you through the comprehensive process, starting from structuring your smart contracts, writing efficient and secure code, compiling using popular development tools, testing for vulnerabilities, and finally deploying contracts to various blockchain environments.

Writing Structured and Maintainable Solidity Code

THE FIRST STEP IN SUCCESSFUL smart contract development involves organizing and structuring your code clearly. The maintainability and readability of smart contracts greatly influence their security and efficiency. Here are the fundamental guidelines for writing structured smart contracts:

- **Single Responsibility Principle (SRP):**

  Each contract should have a specific and singular responsibility. Avoid combining multiple unrelated functionalities in a single contract.

Example of clear contract structuring:

```
pragma solidity ^0.8.0;

// Contract managing user registrations

contract UserRegistry {

mapping(address => bool) public registeredUsers;

function registerUser(address _user) external {

require(!registeredUsers[_user], "Already registered");

registeredUsers[_user] = true;

}
```

```
}

// Contract handling payments separately

contract PaymentProcessor {

function processPayment(address payable _recipient, uint256 _amount) external payable {

require(msg.value == _amount, "Incorrect payment amount");

_recipient.transfer(_amount);

}

}
```

Separating these concerns helps isolate logic, simplify debugging, and reduce risks.

Implementing Solidity Patterns and Standards

UTILIZING WELL-ESTABLISHED design patterns can dramatically improve the robustness of smart contracts. Common Solidity patterns include:

- **Factory Pattern:** Allows dynamic contract creation.
- **Proxy Pattern:** Enables upgradeable contracts.
- **Access Control:** Manages permissioned operations.

Example: Factory Contract Pattern

A Factory Contract is useful when deploying multiple similar contract instances:

```
pragma solidity ^0.8.0;
```

```
contract Wallet {

address public owner;

constructor(address _owner) {

owner = _owner;

}

function withdraw(uint256 amount) external {

require(msg.sender == owner, "Unauthorized");

payable(owner).transfer(amount);

}

}

contract WalletFactory {

Wallet[] public wallets;

function createWallet(address _owner) external {

Wallet wallet = new Wallet(_owner);

wallets.push(wallet);

}

function getWallet(uint index) external view returns (address) {

return address(wallets[index]);

}

}
```

Compiling Smart Contracts

SMART CONTRACTS MUST be compiled to Ethereum Virtual Machine (EVM) bytecode. The compilation also generates an Application Binary Interface (ABI), enabling interaction with contracts. Popular tools for compiling Solidity contracts include:

- **Remix IDE**
- **Truffle Framework**
- **Hardhat**

Compiling with Remix IDE

REMIX IS USER-FRIENDLY and provides real-time compilation:

- Create a new file (MyContract.sol) in Remix IDE.
- Choose the compiler version matching your Solidity pragma statement.
- Click "Compile MyContract.sol" to generate ABI and bytecode.

Compiling with Truffle

INSTALL TRUFFLE GLOBALLY:

npm install -g truffle

Initialize a new project:

truffle init

Inside the contracts folder, add your Solidity file (Example.sol). Compile your contract:

truffle compile

This command compiles your contract and outputs the build artifacts in JSON format under build/contracts.

Compiling with Hardhat

INSTALL HARDHAT:

npm install—save-dev hardhat

npx hardhat

Add contracts to the contracts directory. Compile with:

npx hardhat compile

Testing Solidity Smart Contracts

TESTING ENSURES YOUR contracts behave correctly under various conditions, including edge cases. Common Solidity testing tools include JavaScript frameworks like Mocha and Chai integrated within Truffle or Hardhat.

Example Test with Truffle:

const MyContract = artifacts.require("MyContract");

contract("MyContract", (accounts) => {

let instance;

before(async () => {

```
instance = await MyContract.deployed();

});

it("should deploy with correct initial values", async () => {

const value = await instance.myValue();

assert.equal(value, 0, "Initial value is incorrect");

});

it("should update value correctly", async () => {

await instance.setValue(42);

const updatedValue = await instance.myValue();

assert.equal(updatedValue, 42, "Value not updated correctly");

});

});
```

Run tests using:

```
truffle test
```

Deploying Smart Contracts to Blockchain Networks

AFTER SUCCESSFUL COMPILATION and testing, deploy contracts to blockchain networks. Deployment environments include:

- **Local blockchain (Ganache)**
- **Ethereum Testnets (Goerli, Sepolia, Ropsten)**

- **Mainnet (Ethereum, Polygon, Binance Smart Chain)**

Deploying with Truffle on Ganache (Local Development)

GANACHE IS IDEAL FOR local testing and provides a GUI blockchain simulation. Start Ganache, then:

Configure deployment in truffle-config.js:

```
module.exports = {

networks: {

development: {

host: "127.0.0.1",

port: 8545,

network_id: "*"

}

}

};
```

Deploy your contract:

```
truffle migrate
```

Deploying with Hardhat on Testnets (Goerli)

SETUP HARDHAT NETWORK configuration (hardhat.config.js):

```
module.exports = {
solidity: "0.8.0",
networks: {
goerli: {
url: "https://goerli.infura.io/v3/YOUR_INFURA_PROJECT_ID",
accounts: ["YOUR_PRIVATE_KEY"]
}
}
};
```

Deploy scripts (scripts/deploy.js):

```
async function main() {
const [deployer] = await ethers.getSigners();
const Contract = await ethers.getContractFactory("MyContract");
const contract = await Contract.deploy();
await contract.deployed();
console.log(`Contract deployed at: ${contract.address}`);
}
main().catch((error) => {
console.error(error);
process.exitCode = 1;
```

```
});
```

Deploy with:

```
npx hardhat run scripts/deploy.js—network goerli
```

Deploying Smart Contracts with Remix

USING REMIX IDE IS straightforward:

- Switch environment to Injected Web3 (e.g., MetaMask connected to a testnet).
- Select your contract under "Deploy & Run Transactions."
- Click "Deploy."

Managing Deployed Contracts and Interaction

AFTER DEPLOYMENT, INTERACTING with deployed contracts involves using the ABI and contract address with Web3.js or Ethers.js:

```
const contract = new web3.eth.Contract(ABI, contractAddress);

contract.methods.myFunction().call().then(console.log);
```

Contract Upgradability Strategies

SMART CONTRACTS, BY nature, are immutable once deployed. However, you can achieve controlled upgradability using patterns like the Proxy Pattern:

```
contract ImplementationV1 {
```

```
uint256 public value;
function setValue(uint256 _value) public {
value = _value;
}
}
contract Proxy {
address public implementation;
constructor(address _implementation) {
implementation = _implementation;
}
fallback() external payable {
address impl = implementation;
assembly {
let ptr := mload(0x40)
calldatacopy(ptr, 0, calldatasize())
let result := delegatecall(gas(), impl, ptr, calldatasize(), 0, 0)
let size := returndatasize()
returndatacopy(ptr, 0, size)
switch result
case 0 { revert(ptr, returndatasize()) }
```

```
default { return(ptr, returndatasize()) }
}
}
}
```

By implementing delegate calls, contracts become upgradeable through changing the logic pointer.

Understanding the complete lifecycle of writing, compiling, testing, and deploying smart contracts is essential for professional DApp development. Adhering to these standards and practices will enable you to deploy secure, efficient, and scalable smart contracts ready for production environments.

Gas Optimization and Efficient Smart Contract Development

GAS OPTIMIZATION IS crucial in smart contract development, particularly when deploying contracts on public blockchain networks like Ethereum. Every operation executed within a smart contract consumes gas, which translates directly into ether paid by the user. Efficient code not only saves money but enhances user experience by speeding up transactions. Here, we'll deeply explore various techniques and methodologies to achieve gas-efficient and optimized smart contract code.

Understanding Gas Costs in Ethereum

IN ETHEREUM, "GAS" represents the computational effort required to execute operations within smart contracts. Developers must deeply understand how gas consumption works to optimize smart contracts effectively. Ethereum charges gas based on two parameters:

- **Gas Cost:** Fixed amount per operation (e.g., storage, addition, hashing)
- **Gas Price:** Variable market price of gas (measured in gwei)

Reducing gas consumption means reducing either the number or complexity of operations. Let's examine practical strategies and coding techniques to minimize gas usage.

Minimize Storage Usage

WRITING DATA TO BLOCKCHAIN storage is among the most expensive operations in Ethereum. One efficient approach is minimizing storage usage and utilizing cheaper alternatives such as memory or calldata.

Use memory or calldata over storage:

```
// EXPENSIVE STORAGE example

contract StorageExpensive {

string public message;

function setMessage(string memory newMessage) public {

message = newMessage; // costly

}

}
```

```
// Optimized version using calldata (cheaper)

contract CalldataOptimized {

event MessageUpdated(string newMessage);

function setMessage(string calldata newMessage) external {

emit MessageChanged(newMessage);

}

event MessageChanged(string message);

}
```

By only logging or temporarily storing data, contracts save significantly on gas.

Optimizing Data Structures and Storage Layout

SOLIDITY DATA STRUCTURES can significantly influence gas costs. Developers should carefully choose and structure data.

Efficient Storage Packing

SOLIDITY STORES VARIABLES in storage slots of 256 bits (32 bytes). Packing smaller data types within a single slot saves storage costs:

```
// Inefficient storage packing

contract InefficientPacking {

uint256 a;
```

```
uint128 b;

uint256 c;

}

// Efficient packing example

contract EfficientPacking {

uint128 a;

uint128 b;

uint256 c;

}
```

By arranging small-sized variables closely, you reduce the storage slots used, directly lowering deployment and transaction costs.

Reducing Contract Deployment Costs

CONTRACT DEPLOYMENT is often expensive. By utilizing patterns such as Factory contracts and libraries, developers can substantially reduce deployment overhead.

Library Contracts

LIBRARIES ENCAPSULATE common logic reusable across contracts without redeploying identical code repeatedly:

```
library SafeMath {

function add(uint256 a, uint256 b) internal pure returns (uint256) {

uint256 c = a + b;
```

```
require(c >= a, "Addition overflow");
return c;
}
}
contract UsingLibrary {
using SafeMath for uint256;
uint256 public total;
function increment(uint256 amount) public {
total = total.add(amount); // Using library function
}
}
```

Deploying libraries separately and linking them later reduces bytecode size and deployment costs.

Loop Optimization and Avoiding Excessive Iteration

LOOPS CONSUME CONSIDERABLE gas, especially if iteration is extensive or unpredictable. To optimize loops:

- Limit loop iterations.
- Avoid looping through dynamic arrays without strict upper bounds.

Loop Gas Optimization Example:

INSTEAD OF ITERATING large arrays, consider alternate data structures or off-chain indexing.

Expensive:

```
function findIndex(uint256[] memory array, uint256 target) public pure returns (uint256) {

for (uint256 i = 0; i < array.length; i++) {

if (array[i] == target) {

return i;

}

}

revert("Not found");

}
```

Optimized by using mappings:

```
mapping(uint256 => uint256) public indexMapping;

function setIndex(uint256 target, uint256 index) public {

indexMapping[target] = index;

}

function getIndex(uint256 target) public view returns (uint256) {

require(mappingExists[target], "Not found");

return indexMapping[target];
```

}

Replacing loops with direct mapping lookups significantly reduces execution cost.

Short-circuiting and Conditional Optimization

USING LOGICAL SHORT-circuiting can minimize unnecessary evaluations and reduce gas.

Example without optimization:

```
function checkConditions(uint256 a, uint256 b, uint256 c) public pure returns (bool) {

require(expensiveCheckA(a));

require(expensiveCheckB(b));

return true;

}
```

Optimized with short-circuiting:

```
function optimizedCheck(uint256 a, uint256 b) public pure returns (bool) {

if (!conditionA(a)) return false; // Short-circuit early

if (!conditionB(b)) return false; // Avoid unnecessary checks

return true;

}
```

Early returns or conditional exits help avoid redundant computation, saving significant gas during transactions.

Minimizing External Calls

EXTERNAL CONTRACT CALLS consume additional gas and introduce vulnerability risks. Optimizing calls to external contracts can enhance efficiency.

Minimizing Contract-to-Contract Calls

UNOPTIMIZED CONTRACT interaction:

```
function fetchBalance(address token, address user) external view returns (uint256) {

ERC20 erc20 = ERC20(token);

return erc20.balanceOf(user);

}
```

Optimized caching external call results:

```
contract TokenBalanceChecker {

mapping(address => uint256) balances;

ERC20 erc20;

constructor(address tokenAddress) {

erc20 = ERC20(tokenAddress);

}

function updateBalance(address user) public {
```

```
balances[user] = erc20.balanceOf(user); // Single call cached
}
function getBalance(address user) public view returns (uint256) {
return balances[user];
}
}
```

Reducing frequent external calls by caching responses significantly cuts gas costs and improves execution efficiency.

Gas Optimization Tools and Analyzers

UTILIZE GAS PROFILERS and analyzers to detect inefficiencies in smart contracts. Popular tools include:

- **Eth Gas Reporter:** Provides detailed gas usage reports after testing.
- **Solidity Gas Profiler (with Hardhat):** Offers insights on function-level gas consumption.

Example Eth Gas Reporter with Truffle:

```
npm install eth-gas-reporter—save-dev
```

Modify truffle-config.js:

```
module.exports = {
plugins: ["eth-gas-reporter"],
};
```

Running tests (truffle test) generates a comprehensive gas usage report highlighting inefficient contract functions.

Best Practices Summary for Gas Optimization

- Prioritize using memory/calldata instead of storage.
- Pack variables efficiently to minimize storage.
- Utilize mappings to reduce iteration overhead.
- Reduce deployment cost using libraries and factories.
- Minimize external calls and cache results when possible.
- Avoid expensive computational loops and early terminate whenever possible.
- Use gas profiling tools to continuously refine optimization.

FOLLOWING THESE PRINCIPLES will significantly enhance the efficiency of smart contract development, reduce deployment and transaction costs, and ensure better scalability and performance for decentralized applications in production environments.

Security Best Practices in Smart Contracts

SECURITY IN SMART CONTRACT development is paramount, especially given the irreversible nature of blockchain transactions. Even minor vulnerabilities can lead to significant financial losses and reputational damage. In this extensive section, we'll cover in detail essential security practices and considerations you must integrate into your Solidity smart contract development workflow.

Fundamental Principles of Smart Contract Security

SMART CONTRACT SECURITY revolves around several foundational principles:

- **Immutability:** Once deployed, smart contract code cannot be altered. Thus, rigorous testing and auditing before deployment are critical.

- **Transparency:** All smart contracts are publicly viewable; never store sensitive information.

- **Minimalism:** Code should include only necessary functionality, avoiding overly complex logic that increases vulnerabilities.

- **Fail-safe Design:** Contracts should default to a secure state during unexpected failures.

Common Vulnerabilities and Prevention Techniques

WE'LL DISCUSS IN-DEPTH the common security vulnerabilities found in smart contracts and practical ways to mitigate them.

Reentrancy Attacks

REENTRANCY IS ONE OF the most famous vulnerabilities in Ethereum, responsible for the notorious DAO attack, where attackers repeatedly enter and exploit the contract logic.

Example of vulnerable code:

```
function withdraw(uint256 amount) public {

require(balance[msg.sender] >= amount, "Insufficient funds");

(bool success, ) = msg.sender.call{value: amount}("");

require(success, "Withdrawal failed");

balance[msg.sender] -= amount;

}
```

In the code above, the vulnerability arises because the external call to transfer occurs before the state update.

Mitigation strategy: Implement the **checks-effects-interactions** pattern to protect against reentrancy:

```
mapping(address => uint256) balances;

function safeWithdraw(uint256 amount) external {

require(balances[msg.sender] >= amount, "Insufficient balance"); //
Check

balances[msg.sender] -= amount; // Effects (state changes)

(bool success, ) = msg.sender.call{value: amount}(""); // Interaction

require(success, "Withdrawal failed");

}
```

Here, the balance is updated before interacting with external contracts, eliminating the vulnerability.

Integer Overflow and Underflow

INTEGER OVERFLOW/UNDERFLOW occurs when arithmetic operations exceed their limits, resulting in unexpected contract behavior.

Example of vulnerable code:

```
uint8 public count = 255;

function increment() public {

count += 1; // Causes overflow, resets to 0

}
```

Mitigation strategy: Solidity ≥ 0.8.0 automatically reverts transactions on integer overflow/underflow. For older versions, explicitly use libraries like SafeMath:

```
import "@openzeppelin/contracts/utils/math/SafeMath.sol";

contract SafeContract {

using SafeMath for uint256;

uint256 public totalSupply;

function increaseSupply(uint256 amount) public {

totalSupply = totalSupply.add(amount); // Safe addition

}

}
```

Access Control Issues

IMPROPERLY IMPLEMENTED access control allows unauthorized users to perform sensitive operations.

Example of weak access control:

```
function withdrawFunds() public {
payable(msg.sender).transfer(address(this).balance);
}
```

Anyone can call the function and withdraw all funds.

Mitigation strategy: Explicit access control using modifiers:

```
address private owner;
modifier onlyOwner {
require(msg.sender == owner, "Unauthorized");
_;
}
function withdrawAll() external onlyOwner {
payable(owner).transfer(address(this).balance);
}
```

Front-Running Attacks

FRONT-RUNNING INVOLVES manipulating transactions in the mempool by exploiting transaction ordering. Common in decentralized exchanges or auctions.

Mitigation techniques:

- Use commit-reveal schemes to prevent sensitive information leakage.
- Utilize decentralized exchanges' AMM (Automated Market Maker) algorithms to minimize manipulation.

Example of commit-reveal scheme to mitigate front-running:

```
mapping(address => bytes32) public commitments;

function commit(bytes32 hash) external {

commitments[msg.sender] = hash;

}

function reveal(string memory secret) external {

require(commitments[msg.sender] == keccak256(abi.encodePacked(secret)), "Invalid reveal");

// Execute logic securely

}
```

Security in Smart Contract Development Lifecycle

SECURITY MUST BE INTEGRATED into every stage of the smart contract lifecycle:

Development Phase

- Implement security best practices and patterns discussed previously.

- Conduct thorough code reviews and pair programming sessions.

Compilation and Static Analysis

- Use linters and static analysis tools (e.g., Slither, Mythril, Solidity Security Scanner) to automatically detect potential vulnerabilities.

EXAMPLE OF RUNNING Slither:

```
slither ./contracts/MyContract.sol
```

Slither will return detailed warnings highlighting potential risks in your codebase.

Testing and Dynamic Analysis

- Use fuzz testing with tools like Echidna to uncover vulnerabilities through randomized inputs.
- Write comprehensive unit and integration tests covering edge cases.

Using OpenZeppelin for Enhanced Security

LEVERAGING WELL-ESTABLISHED, community-tested libraries significantly improves smart contract security. OpenZeppelin contracts provide secure implementations of common patterns.

Example usage of OpenZeppelin's Ownable contract:

```
import "@openzeppelin/contracts/access/Ownable.sol";
```

```
contract MySecureContract is Ownable {

function secureWithdrawal(address payable recipient, uint256 amount) external onlyOwner {

recipient.transfer(amount);

}

}
```

The Ownable pattern automatically provides secure, tested, and audited ownership management.

Implementing Circuit Breakers and Emergency Stops

CIRCUIT BREAKERS OR pausing mechanisms allow developers to stop contract execution temporarily if vulnerabilities or unexpected events occur:

```
bool public paused = false;

modifier whenNotPaused() {

require(!paused, "Paused");

_;

}

function pause() external onlyOwner {

paused = true;

}

function unpause() external onlyOwner {

paused = false;
```

```
}
function sensitiveOperation() external whenNotPaused {
// sensitive code here
}
```

Secure Deployment and Upgrade Management

SECURE DEPLOYMENT INVOLVES several critical steps, including environment verification, network choice, and robust key management.

Multi-Signature Deployment

TO ENHANCE DEPLOYMENT security, consider multisig wallets requiring multiple signatures before execution:

- Tools like Gnosis Safe manage sensitive operations with multi-signature schemes.

Secure Contract Upgrade Strategies

IF UPGRADEABILITY IS essential, implement secure upgrade patterns like proxy contracts:

```
contract LogicContract {
uint256 public value;
function setValue(uint256 _value) external {
value = _value;
}
```

```
}
contract ProxyContract {
address public implementation;
address private owner;
modifier onlyOwner {
require(msg.sender == owner, "Unauthorized");
_;
}
constructor(address _implementation) {
implementation = _implementation;
owner = msg.sender;
}
function upgradeImplementation(address newImplementation) external onlyOwner {
implementation = newImplementation;
}
fallback() external payable {
address impl = implementation;
assembly {
let ptr := mload(0x40)
calldatacopy(ptr, 0, calldatasize())
```

```
let result := delegatecall(gas(), impl, ptr, calldatasize(), 0, 0)

let size := returndatasize()

returndatacopy(ptr, 0, size)

switch result

case 0 { revert(ptr, size) }

default { return(ptr, size) }

}

}

}
```

This strategy allows updating logic contracts securely without losing contract state.

Regulatory and Compliance Considerations

SECURITY ISN'T JUST about technical details; legal and compliance considerations also apply. Consider factors such as GDPR compliance, financial regulations (for DeFi applications), and jurisdictional laws governing smart contracts.

Security Audits and Reviews

BEFORE DEPLOYING CONTRACTS to mainnet, thorough security audits by experienced professionals or reputable auditing firms are essential. Auditors analyze contracts using:

- **Static code analysis**
- **Dynamic code execution tests**

- **Manual code reviews**

Integrating audit findings is critical. Always conduct post-audit refactoring and retest extensively after modifications.

Security Best Practice Summary

- Always implement **checks-effects-interactions** to avoid reentrancy.
- Enforce clear access control policies using modifiers.
- Validate and sanitize inputs rigorously.
- Utilize reliable libraries and secure standards (e.g., OpenZeppelin).
- Regularly conduct comprehensive security audits.
- Continuously monitor deployed contracts for anomalies.
- Educate the development team consistently about security best practices.

BY RIGOROUSLY APPLYING these strategies, Solidity developers can significantly minimize vulnerabilities, reduce financial risk, and ensure high-quality, robust smart contract development that users can trust with their assets and sensitive data.

Chapter 5: Building the Backend for DApps

The Role of Decentralized Storage (IPFS, Arweave)

IN TRADITIONAL WEB applications, data storage typically relies on centralized servers, creating single points of failure, vulnerability to censorship, and potential for unauthorized access or manipulation. Decentralized applications (DApps), however, emphasize distributed and secure storage to maintain transparency, security, and immutability. Decentralized storage solutions like the InterPlanetary File System (IPFS) and Arweave have become essential components in the modern DApp backend architecture.

Introduction to Decentralized Storage Systems

DECENTRALIZED STORAGE systems use peer-to-peer (P2P) technology, enabling data distribution across multiple nodes. This removes reliance on centralized hosting providers like AWS, Google Cloud, or Azure, significantly enhancing data resilience and integrity. Key features of decentralized storage solutions include:

- **Immutability:** Data stored is cryptographically hashed and cannot be altered without changing its hash value.
- **Availability:** Data remains accessible even if certain nodes fail or are removed from the network.
- **Transparency:** Data availability is public, providing verifiable proof of storage and retrieval.

- **Resistance to Censorship:** Without central control, data cannot easily be censored or blocked.

Understanding IPFS (InterPlanetary File System)

IPFS IS A DISTRIBUTED file system designed to make the web faster, safer, and more open. It replaces traditional location-based addressing (URLs pointing to servers) with content-based addressing (hashes pointing directly to the content itself).

Content-Based Addressing

IPFS USES CRYPTOGRAPHIC hashes generated by the content itself as unique identifiers called Content Identifiers (CIDs). This ensures immutability; changing even one byte of data results in an entirely different CID.

Example of CID generation:

```
echo "Hello, IPFS!" > file.txt

ipfs add file.txt
```

The output might look like this:

```
added QmTm8uQn5BqR... file.txt
```

This CID (QmTm8uQn5BqR...) can now directly fetch the stored content from any node in the IPFS network.

IPFS Architecture and Components

IPFS RELIES ON SEVERAL critical components:

- **Libp2p:** A modular network stack that handles peer discovery, communication, and security protocols.
- **Merkle DAG:** IPFS structures files into Merkle Directed Acyclic Graphs (DAGs), enabling efficient content verification and retrieval.
- **Distributed Hash Table (DHT):** Facilitates quick and efficient content discovery across the network.

Practical Implementation of IPFS for DApps

Installing and Setting up IPFS

TO BEGIN USING IPFS in your DApp backend, first install the IPFS daemon:

```
# Installation on Ubuntu

sudo apt-get update

sudo apt-get install ipfs
```

Then initialize IPFS:

```
ipfs init
```

Storing and Retrieving Data

FILES ARE ADDED TO IPFS using:

```
ipfs add <file_name>
```

To retrieve files:

```
ipfs get <CID>
```

Integrating IPFS with Smart Contracts

SMART CONTRACTS ON Ethereum or other blockchains store minimal data due to gas costs. To manage larger datasets (e.g., images, documents), IPFS can be used. Typically, a contract only stores the CID, significantly reducing storage costs.

Example Solidity contract referencing an IPFS hash:

```
pragma solidity ^0.8.0;

contract IPFSStorage {

mapping(address => string) public userFiles;

function storeFileHash(string memory cid) public {

userFiles[msg.sender] = cid;

}

function retrieveFileHash(address user) public view returns (string memory) {

return userFiles[user];

}

}
```

The frontend retrieves the IPFS hash from the blockchain, using a library like Web3.js, then fetches the content from IPFS.

Limitations and Considerations of IPFS

WHILE IPFS PROVIDES robust decentralized storage, it is not without challenges:

- **Data Availability:** IPFS nodes only host data they have pinned or accessed, potentially causing content availability issues if nodes remove or stop pinning data.

- **Performance:** Content retrieval speeds can vary significantly depending on node availability and network latency.

- **Incentive Mechanisms:** IPFS does not inherently reward participants for storage or bandwidth, though platforms like Filecoin layer economic incentives over IPFS to solve this.

Persistent and Permanent Storage with Arweave

ARWEAVE PRESENTS AN alternative focused on permanent data storage through a unique blockchain-like structure, termed the "blockweave," specifically designed for long-term data preservation.

How Arweave Works

ARWEAVE UTILIZES PROOF of Access (PoA), a consensus mechanism requiring miners to prove they can retrieve historical data, incentivizing data permanence. Unlike IPFS, Arweave includes built-in incentives and economic guarantees to maintain data indefinitely.

Key Arweave features:

- **Permanent Storage:** Data stored once is available permanently, without recurring fees.

- **Pay-Once Model:** Users pay a one-time fee for permanent storage, calculated based on file size and storage demand.

Setting up Arweave for DApps

ARWEAVE INTEGRATION typically uses its JavaScript SDK (arweave-js):

npm install arweave

Example code to upload files to Arweave:

```
import Arweave from 'arweave';

const arweave = Arweave.init({

host: 'arweave.net',

port: 443,

protocol: 'https'

});

async function uploadData(data) {

let transaction = await arweave.createTransaction({ data });

await arweave.transactions.sign(transaction);

let response = await arweave.transactions.post(transaction);

console.log(transaction.id); // Arweave transaction ID, similar to CID

}
```

Arweave and Smart Contract Integration

LIKE IPFS, SMART CONTRACTS typically store Arweave transaction IDs rather than large files. The smart contract thus becomes cost-efficient and maintains transparency.

Example Solidity integration:

```
pragma solidity ^0.8.0;

contract ArweaveStorage {

mapping(address => string) public userData;

function storeData(string memory txId) public {

userData[msg.sender] = txId;

}

function getData(address user) public view returns (string memory)
{

return userData[user];

}

}
```

This approach keeps gas costs minimal and leverages Arweave's robust permanent storage.

Choosing Between IPFS and Arweave for Your DApp

WHEN DESIGNING THE backend, consider the following criteria:

Criterion	IPFS	Arweave
Data Permanence	Requires pinning solutions	Built-in permanent storage
Economic Model	Typically free, incentivized via Filecoin	One-time fee for permanent storage
Data Retrieval Speed	Variable; depends on node availability	Generally consistent and predictable
Ideal Use Cases	Short-term file availability, large files, general-purpose storage	Permanent storage, legal documents, NFTs, historical records

IPFS suits applications needing rapid prototyping or temporary storage with lower initial costs. Arweave suits long-term, permanent, and verifiable data storage, ideal for NFTs, legal documentation, or historical records.

Ensuring Security and Reliability in Decentralized Storage

WHEN IMPLEMENTING DECENTRALIZED storage solutions, consider the following best practices:

- **Pinning Services:** Use IPFS pinning services (Pinata, Infura) to maintain availability.
- **Regular Backups:** Always maintain backups of your data off-chain.
- **Encryption:** Store sensitive information encrypted; decentralized storage is public and transparent.
- **Monitoring and Alerts:** Implement monitoring services to check file availability and accessibility.

Conclusion

DECENTRALIZED STORAGE solutions such as IPFS and Arweave represent critical building blocks for DApp infrastructure. IPFS offers flexible, location-independent storage, while Arweave provides guaranteed permanent data preservation. Choosing the appropriate decentralized storage depends on your DApp's goals, data permanence needs, economic considerations, and intended use cases. Ultimately, effective backend integration of decentralized storage enhances DApp resilience, transparency, and reliability, supporting the broader adoption of decentralized technologies in the digital ecosystem.

Connecting Smart Contracts with Web3.js and Ethers.js

TO BUILD FULLY FUNCTIONAL decentralized applications (DApps), the integration of smart contracts with frontend and backend systems is crucial. Two dominant JavaScript libraries—Web3.js and Ethers.js—facilitate interaction between DApps and Ethereum-based smart contracts, enabling developers to write efficient and scalable backend logic.

Understanding Web3.js and Ethers.js

Web3.js

WEB3.JS IS THE ETHEREUM JavaScript API that allows applications to communicate with the Ethereum blockchain. It is widely adopted, extensively documented, and suitable for diverse development scenarios. Web3.js enables developers to perform tasks such as sending transactions, reading smart contract states, and managing Ethereum accounts directly within their JavaScript applications.

Install Web3.js using npm:

```
npm install web3
```

Ethers.js

ETHERS.JS IS A MORE modern and streamlined alternative to Web3.js, providing similar functionalities but with a simpler, cleaner API. Ethers.js supports various Ethereum operations, including wallet creation, transaction handling, contract interaction, and event listening.

Install Ethers.js via npm:

```
npm install ethers
```

Setting Up a Connection to the Ethereum Blockchain

Establishing Connections with Web3.js

TO ESTABLISH A CONNECTION to the Ethereum network, you must specify an Ethereum node provider (e.g., Infura or Alchemy). Below is an example of how to connect to Ethereum using Web3.js:

```
const Web3 = require('web3');

const web3 = new Web3('https://mainnet.infura.io/v3/YOUR_INFURA_PROJECT_ID');

async function getLatestBlockNumber() {
```

```
const latestBlockNumber = await web3.eth.getBlockNumber();

console.log('Latest Block:', latestBlockNumber);

}

getLatestBlockNumber();
```

Establishing Connections with Ethers.js

WITH ETHERS.JS, CONNECTING to Ethereum is equally straightforward:

```
const { ethers } = require('ethers');

const provider = new ethers.providers.InfuraProvider('mainnet', 'YOUR_INFURA_PROJECT_ID');

async function getLatestBlockNumber() {

const latestBlockNumber = await provider.getBlockNumber();

console.log('Latest Block:', latestBlockNumber);

}

getLatestBlockNumber();
```

Interacting with Smart Contracts

TO INTERACT WITH SMART contracts, you first need the contract's ABI (Application Binary Interface) and deployed address. The ABI defines available methods and events on the smart contract, facilitating JavaScript-based interactions.

Contract Interaction Using Web3.js

HERE'S AN EXAMPLE USING Web3.js to interact with a simple ERC-20 token contract to retrieve account balances:

```
const Web3 = require('web3');

const web3 = new Web3('https://mainnet.infura.io/v3/YOUR_INFURA_PROJECT_ID');

const tokenABI = [/* ERC-20 ABI here */];

const tokenAddress = '0xTokenContractAddress';

const contract = new web3.eth.Contract(tokenABI, tokenAddress);

async function getBalance(address) {

const balance = await contract.methods.balanceOf(address).call();

console.log(`Balance of ${address}:`, web3.utils.fromWei(balance, 'ether'));

}

getBalance('0xYourEthereumAddress');
```

Contract Interaction Using Ethers.js

THE SAME EXAMPLE USING Ethers.js looks like this:

```
const { ethers } = require('ethers');

const provider = new ethers.providers.InfuraProvider('mainnet', 'YOUR_INFURA_PROJECT_ID');

const tokenABI = [/* ERC-20 ABI here */];
```

```
const tokenAddress = '0xTokenContractAddress';

const contract = new ethers.Contract(tokenAddress, tokenABI, provider);

async function getBalance(address) {

const balance = await contract.balanceOf(address);

console.log(`Balance of ${address}:`, ethers.utils.formatEther(balance));

}

getBalance('0xYourEthereumAddress');
```

Sending Transactions to Smart Contracts

SENDING TRANSACTIONS requires a signer, typically a private key, to authorize contract modifications.

Sending Transactions with Web3.js

EXAMPLE OF SENDING a transaction with Web3.js:

```
const Web3 = require('web3');

const web3 = new Web3('https://mainnet.infura.io/v3/YOUR_INFURA_PROJECT_ID');

const account = web3.eth.accounts.privateKeyToAccount('YOUR_PRIVATE_KEY');

web3.eth.accounts.wallet.add(account);

const contract = new web3.eth.Contract(tokenABI, tokenAddress);
```

```
async function transferTokens(toAddress, amount) {

const tx = contract.methods.transfer(toAddress, web3.utils.toWei(amount, 'ether'));

const gas = await tx.estimateGas({ from: account.address });

const gasPrice = await web3.eth.getGasPrice();

const receipt = await tx.send({

from: account.address,

gas,

gasPrice

});

console.log('Transaction successful:', receipt.transactionHash);

}

transferTokens('0xRecipientAddress', '10');
```

Sending Transactions with Ethers.js

THE EQUIVALENT IN ETHERS.js is simpler:

```
const { ethers } = require('ethers');

const provider = new ethers.providers.InfuraProvider('mainnet', 'YOUR_INFURA_PROJECT_ID');

const wallet = new ethers.Wallet('YOUR_PRIVATE_KEY', provider);
```

```
const contract = new ethers.Contract(tokenAddress, tokenABI, wallet);

async function transferTokens(toAddress, amount) {

const tx = await contract.transfer(toAddress, ethers.utils.parseEther(amount));

console.log('Transaction sent:', tx.hash);

await tx.wait();

console.log('Transaction confirmed:', tx.hash);

}

transferTokens('0xRecipientAddress', '10');
```

Listening to Contract Events

LISTENING TO SMART contract events enables real-time responses within your DApp backend.

Event Listening with Web3.js

HERE'S HOW YOU LISTEN for an event:

```
contract.events.Transfer({

fromBlock: 'latest'

})

.on('data', event => {

console.log('New Transfer:', event.returnValues);

})
```

.on('error', error => {

console.error('Error:', error);

});

Event Listening with Ethers.js

EVENT LISTENING IN Ethers.js:

contract.on('Transfer', (from, to, amount, event) => {

console.log(`Transfer from ${from} to ${to} of ${ethers.utils.formatEther(amount)} tokens.`);

});

Handling Common Errors and Edge Cases

BOTH LIBRARIES ENCOUNTER common issues such as network connectivity errors, incorrect ABI/address references, insufficient funds, and gas estimation issues.

Best Practices:

- Always handle promises and asynchronous calls gracefully with try-catch blocks.
- Validate contract addresses and ABIs thoroughly before deploying to production.
- Implement retries and exponential backoff when handling network errors or failed transactions.

Security Considerations

WHEN INTEGRATING WEB3.js and Ethers.js into your backend:

- **Never expose private keys:** Always store private keys securely in environment variables or dedicated secure key management services (e.g., AWS KMS, Hashicorp Vault).
- **Rate Limiting and IP Whitelisting:** Secure your DApp's backend infrastructure from DDoS attacks or malicious usage by implementing appropriate middleware.
- **Use dedicated signer servers:** Maintain separate servers for signing transactions, minimizing exposure of sensitive operations.

Choosing Between Web3.js and Ethers.js

BOTH LIBRARIES HAVE strengths suited for specific development scenarios:

Criteria	Web3.js	Ethers.js
Community & Popularity	Large and mature	Rapidly growing, actively maintained
API Simplicity	Verbose but clear	Concise and streamlined
Documentation	Extensive but sometimes outdated	Clear and easy to follow
TypeScript Support	Good (recently improved)	Excellent native TypeScript support
Performance	Robust, slightly heavier	Lightweight, optimized for speed
Ideal Use	Complex, enterprise DApps	Simplified modern DApp development

Conclusion

WEB3.JS AND ETHERS.js both provide robust solutions for integrating smart contracts with your backend. Web3.js excels in flexibility and familiarity within the blockchain ecosystem, while Ethers.js emphasizes developer friendliness, simplicity, and performance. By understanding their strengths and trade-offs, you can select the optimal library for your specific DApp backend requirements, ensuring efficient and secure integration for your decentralized applications.

Developing Secure and Scalable Backend Infrastructure

IN DECENTRALIZED APPLICATION (DApp) development, the backend serves as the critical infrastructure connecting smart contracts, blockchain nodes, decentralized storage, user authentication mechanisms, and frontend interfaces. This infrastructure must prioritize not only scalability and efficiency but also robust security. A well-designed backend ensures reliable operation, resilience against attacks, and scalability that meets the needs of a growing user base.

Architecture Considerations for Secure DApp Backends

WHEN PLANNING BACKEND infrastructure for decentralized applications, the architecture significantly impacts security, scalability, and maintainability. Here are essential components to consider:

Modular Design

A MODULAR BACKEND ARCHITECTURE simplifies upgrades, debugging, and scalability. Segregate distinct backend functionalities such as user authentication, blockchain interaction, data storage, and API management into separate, reusable modules or microservices.

- **Example Architecture Structure:**

  ○ Authentication Layer (MetaMask, WalletConnect, custom JWT implementations)

  ○ API Gateway (REST or GraphQL APIs)

  ○ Smart Contract Interaction Layer (Web3.js or Ethers.js)

  ○ Decentralized Storage Access Layer (IPFS, Arweave)

  ○ Security and Monitoring Layer (logging, alerting, auditing)

Serverless Infrastructure

SERVERLESS COMPUTING frameworks, like AWS Lambda or Azure Functions, enhance scalability and reduce operational overhead. Serverless solutions reduce attack surfaces by eliminating unnecessary infrastructure management, automatically scaling services based on usage, and improving cost efficiency through pay-per-execution billing models.

Example of a simple AWS Lambda function to interact with a smart contract using Ethers.js:

```
const { ethers } = require('ethers');

exports.handler = async (event) => {

const provider = new ethers.providers.InfuraProvider('mainnet', process.env.INFURA_API_KEY);

const wallet = new ethers.Wallet(process.env.PRIVATE_KEY, provider);

const contract = new ethers.Contract(process.env.CONTRACT_ADDRESS, CONTRACT_ABI, wallet);

try {

const response = await contract.someMethod(event.arguments);

return {

statusCode: 200,

body: JSON.stringify({ success: true, data: response }),

};
```

```
} catch (error) {
console.error(error);
return {
statusCode: 500,
body: JSON.stringify({ error: 'Contract interaction failed' }),
};
}
};
```

Microservices Approach

USING MICROSERVICES, each backend component runs as a separate service, interacting through APIs. For example, authentication, smart contract transactions, logging, and frontend APIs could run independently. This approach provides greater flexibility in updating and scaling parts of the system independently.

Security Best Practices in Backend Development

SECURITY IS PARAMOUNT in decentralized applications due to their immutable nature and direct financial interactions. Here are best practices for creating secure backend systems:

Environment Variables and Secret Management

STORE SENSITIVE CREDENTIALS and API keys securely. Avoid embedding secrets directly in the source code. Instead, use environment variables, dedicated secrets management systems (AWS Secrets Manager, HashiCorp Vault), or encrypted CI/CD pipelines.

Example .env configuration:

```
PRIVATE_KEY=your-private-key

INFURA_API_KEY=your-infura-api-key

DATABASE_URL=your-database-connection-string
```

Accessing environment variables securely in Node.js:

```
require('dotenv').config();

const privateKey = process.env.PRIVATE_KEY;
```

Data Validation and Sanitization

ALWAYS VALIDATE INPUT data rigorously. Implement strict validation rules to avoid injection attacks and malicious inputs. For example, with Express.js backend API:

```
const express = require('express');

const Joi = require('joi');

const router = express.Router();

const schema = Joi.object({

address: Joi.string().regex(/^0x[a-fA-F0-9]{40}$/).required(),

amount: Joi.number().positive().required(),

});

router.post('/transfer', async (req, res) => {
```

```
const { error, value } = schema.validate(req.body);

if (error) return res.status(400).json({ error: error.details[0].message
});

// Safe to process transaction here

});
```

Logging and Monitoring

IMPLEMENT COMPREHENSIVE logging and monitoring tools to maintain visibility into application performance and security. Services like AWS CloudWatch, ELK Stack, Grafana, and Prometheus are invaluable. Proper logging can detect suspicious activities early.

Implementing Robust Security Practices

THE DECENTRALIZED NATURE of DApps magnifies the importance of robust backend security. Consider the following critical practices to mitigate vulnerabilities:

Input Validation and Sanitization

ALL INPUTS FROM USER interfaces, APIs, or external services must be validated and sanitized to avoid injection attacks or malformed data.

Authentication and Authorization

EVEN THOUGH BLOCKCHAIN authentication involves cryptographic wallet signatures, backend APIs must still verify request authenticity. For example, ensure that users are authorized to trigger smart contract interactions or access protected resources.

Sample verification with a signed message:

```
const { ethers } = require('ethers');

async function verifySignature(message, signature, address) {

const signerAddress = ethers.utils.verifyMessage(message, signature);

return signerAddress.toLowerCase() === address.toLowerCase();

}
```

Scalability in DApp Backend Infrastructure

TO ENSURE YOUR DAPP scales efficiently, carefully plan infrastructure from the start:

Horizontal Scaling

ARCHITECT YOUR BACKEND to horizontally scale by deploying multiple instances behind load balancers or using serverless functions to handle increasing loads seamlessly.

Database and Caching Strategies

WHILE DECENTRALIZED storage manages larger datasets, centralized databases (MongoDB, PostgreSQL) are often used for user data, analytics, or quick indexing. Utilize caching (Redis, Memcached) to minimize blockchain queries, enhancing performance.

Example caching with Redis:

```
const redis = require('redis');

const client = redis.createClient();

async function cacheContractData(key, data) {

await client.setex(key, 3600, JSON.stringify(data));

}

async function getCachedData(key) {

const data = await client.get(key);

if (data) {

return JSON.parse(data);

} else {

// query blockchain or IPFS and cache it

}

}
```

API Rate Limiting and Protection

PROTECT YOUR BACKEND APIs with rate limiting (Express-rate-limit), preventing denial-of-service attacks and controlling API resource usage:

```
const rateLimit = require('express-rate-limit');

app.use(rateLimit({
```

```
windowMs: 15 * 60 * 1000, // 15 minutes

max: 100,

message: 'Too many requests, please slow down.',

}));
```

Scalability Through Layer 2 Solutions and Off-chain Data

MANY DAPPS INCORPORATE Layer 2 scaling solutions (Polygon, Arbitrum) to handle increased user loads. In backend architecture, smart contracts on Layer 2 chains require similar integrations with Web3.js/Ethers.js. Consider using off-chain data indexing solutions (The Graph or Moralis) to efficiently query blockchain events without direct node interaction, significantly improving response times.

Compliance and Regulatory Considerations

REGULATORY COMPLIANCE is increasingly critical for DApps operating within specific jurisdictions. Integrate compliance measures such as:

- User data management adhering to GDPR, CCPA.
- Transaction compliance with KYC and AML practices where necessary.
- Clear audit trails and logs for transparency and compliance.

Continuous Integration and Deployment (CI/CD)

A ROBUST CI/CD PIPELINE accelerates development cycles and strengthens security. Integrate automated tests (unit, integration, end-to-end), static code analysis (ESLint, SonarQube), and security vulnerability scans (Snyk, Dependabot).

Sample GitHub Actions workflow:

```
name: CI/CD Pipeline

on:

push:

branches: [main, develop]

jobs:

build:

runs-on: ubuntu-latest

steps:

- uses: actions/checkout@v3

- name: Install dependencies

run: npm install

- name: Run tests

run: npm test

- name: Deploy

if: github.ref == 'refs/heads/main'
```

```
run: |
npm run build
npm run deploy
```

Disaster Recovery and High Availability

A SCALABLE AND SECURE backend demands redundancy to withstand failures. Implement disaster recovery strategies such as:

- Regular snapshots of critical data.
- Geographic distribution of services to prevent single-region outages.
- Automated failover mechanisms.

Scalability: Planning for Growth

YOUR DAPP BACKEND MUST anticipate user growth. Design with scalability in mind:

- Choose technologies that scale horizontally (Docker containers, Kubernetes clusters).
- Consider Layer 2 or cross-chain architectures to expand user capacity.
- Monitor system performance continuously and optimize bottlenecks.

Conclusion

DEVELOPING SECURE AND scalable backend infrastructure for DApps requires careful planning across architecture, security, performance optimization, and deployment practices. Incorporating modular design, secure storage of private keys, comprehensive logging, robust error handling, rate limiting, and continuous monitoring dramatically strengthens your backend infrastructure. By leveraging modern tooling (Web3.js, Ethers.js), layer 2 solutions, decentralized storage, and established cloud technologies, you ensure reliability, security, and scalability that users expect in a modern, high-performance decentralized application.

Interacting with Oracles and Off-Chain Data

DECENTRALIZED APPLICATIONS (DApps) running on blockchains, such as Ethereum, are inherently secure and transparent, but they face significant challenges when attempting to access external or off-chain data. This limitation arises from blockchain environments' deterministic nature: smart contracts cannot directly query real-world data sources or APIs due to inherent security constraints. To bridge the gap between on-chain logic and off-chain information, developers integrate oracle services, enabling smart contracts to securely consume external data, thereby vastly expanding their functionality.

Understanding Oracles and Their Significance in DApps

ORACLES SERVE AS TRUSTED data providers that bridge the gap between blockchain-based smart contracts and external data sources. They allow smart contracts to interact securely with off-chain resources like market prices, sports outcomes, weather data, real-world events, and much more. Oracles provide verifiable data inputs crucial for decentralized finance (DeFi) protocols, insurance applications, prediction markets, gaming, and supply chain tracking.

Types of Blockchain Oracles

BLOCKCHAIN ORACLES can be categorized broadly as:

- **Software Oracles**: Retrieve online data like prices, API responses, or external database queries.

- **Hardware Oracles:** Fetch data from IoT sensors or hardware devices.

- **Inbound Oracles:** Provide off-chain data to on-chain smart contracts.

- **Outbound Oracles:** Deliver smart contract data to off-chain systems.

- **Centralized vs. Decentralized Oracles:** Centralized oracles rely on single data sources, while decentralized oracles aggregate information from multiple sources, enhancing security and reliability.

Popular Oracle Solutions

SEVERAL ORACLE SOLUTIONS have emerged, each serving unique scenarios and requirements. Prominent examples include Chainlink, Band Protocol, API3, and Tellor.

Chainlink Oracle

CHAINLINK IS THE MOST widely adopted decentralized oracle network, extensively used within Ethereum-based DeFi projects. It aggregates data from multiple nodes, ensuring accurate, tamper-resistant information.

Integrating Chainlink Oracle with Smart Contracts

CHAINLINK IS THE INDUSTRY standard for decentralized oracle services, known for providing reliable price feeds, randomness, and external API integration.

Setting Up Chainlink in Solidity:

INSTALL CHAINLINK INTERFACES in your project:

```
npm install @chainlink/contracts
```

A simple smart contract example fetching ETH/USD price using Chainlink:

```
pragma solidity ^0.8.0;

import "@chainlink/contracts/src/v0.8/interfaces/AggregatorV3Interface.sol";

contract PriceConsumer {

AggregatorV3Interface internal priceFeed;

constructor() {

// ETH/USD price feed contract on Ethereum mainnet

priceFeed = AggregatorV3Interface(0x694AA1769357215DE4FAC081bf1f309aD(

}

function getLatestPrice() public view returns (int256) {

(,int256 price,,,) = priceFeed.latestRoundData();
```

```
return price;

}

}
```

This contract securely retrieves ETH/USD pricing information without relying on external APIs directly.

Retrieving Data in Your DApp Frontend (Ethers.js):

```
CONST { ETHERS } = require('ethers');

const provider = new ethers.providers.InfuraProvider('mainnet', 'YOUR_INFURA_API_KEY');

const aggregatorV3InterfaceABI = [/* Chainlink Aggregator ABI here */];

const priceFeedAddress = '0x694AA1769357215DE4FAC081bf1f309aDC325306';

async function getPrice() {

const priceFeed = new ethers.Contract(priceFeedAddress, aggregatorV3InterfaceABI, provider);

const roundData = await priceFeed.latestRoundData();

const decimals = await priceFeed.decimals();

const price = ethers.utils.formatUnits(roundData.answer, decimals);

console.log('ETH/USD:', price);

}

getLatestPrice();
```

Chainlink ensures that your DApp's financial data is reliable and tamper-proof, essential in DeFi applications like lending protocols, stablecoins, and decentralized exchanges.

Custom Oracles and API Integration

SOMETIMES STANDARD oracle solutions like Chainlink might not cover niche or specialized data. In such cases, developing a custom oracle can provide precise data to your DApp.

Creating a Custom Oracle using Oraclize (Provable):

PROVABLE (FORMERLY Oraclize) provides custom oracle solutions for specialized API interactions.

Solidity Integration:

```
PRAGMA SOLIDITY ^0.8.0;

import "github.com/provable-things/ethereum-api/provableAPI.sol";

contract CustomOracleExample is usingProvable {

string public data;

event LogNewProvableQuery(string description);

event LogNewData(string result);

function requestData() public payable {

emit LogNewProvableQuery("Provable query sent; awaiting response...");
```

```
provable_query("URL", "json(https://api.example.com/data).field");

}

function __callback(bytes32 _queryId, string memory _result) public override {

require(msg.sender == provable_cbAddress());

data = _result;

emit LogNewData(_result);

}

}
```

Custom oracles provide flexibility to access APIs tailored specifically for your application's needs, such as proprietary or specialized data sources.

Risks and Security Considerations with Oracles

INTERACTING WITH EXTERNAL data introduces significant risks, including oracle manipulation, inaccurate data, front running, and flash-loan attacks. Protecting your smart contracts against these vulnerabilities requires careful design:

- **Data Manipulation:** Utilize decentralized oracle networks (like Chainlink) to mitigate the risk of manipulated data.
- **Oracle Redundancy:** Use multiple oracles or aggregated feeds to minimize single points of failure.

- **Time and Data Validation:** Include sanity checks within your smart contracts (e.g., timestamps, thresholds, and limits).

Using Oracles in Decentralized Finance (DeFi)

ORACLES ARE VITAL IN DeFi applications for maintaining accurate, timely, and trustworthy financial data.

Examples in DeFi:

- **Collateralized Lending Platforms:** Price feeds determine collateral valuation, enabling accurate collateralization ratios (e.g., MakerDAO, Compound).

- **Stablecoins:** Protocols like DAI rely on oracles to monitor asset prices and maintain stability.

- **Prediction Markets and Insurance:** Depend heavily on trustworthy external event outcomes provided via oracles.

Off-chain Computation and Hybrid Smart Contracts

BEYOND DATA PROVISION, modern oracle networks (e.g., Chainlink Keepers, Chainlink Functions) can execute computations off-chain and deliver verified results on-chain, creating efficient and cost-effective hybrid smart contracts.

Chainlink Keepers Integration Example:

```
PRAGMA SOLIDITY ^0.8.0;

interface KeeperCompatibleInterface {
```

```
function checkUpkeep(bytes calldata checkData) external returns
(bool upkeepNeeded, bytes memory performData);

function performUpkeep(bytes calldata performData) external;

}

contract Counter is KeeperCompatibleInterface {

uint public counter;

uint public lastTimeStamp;

constructor() {

lastTimeStamp = block.timestamp;

counter = 0;

}

function checkUpkeep(bytes calldata) external view override returns
(bool upkeepNeeded) {

upkeepNeeded = (block.timestamp - lastTimeStamp) > 1 days;

}

function performUpkeep(bytes calldata) external override {

if ((block.timestamp - lastTimeStamp) > 1 days) {

counter++;

lastTimeStamp = block.timestamp;

}

}
```

```
}
```

This hybrid model significantly reduces on-chain costs and enhances smart contract capabilities.

Decentralized Oracles and DAO Integration

DECENTRALIZED AUTONOMOUS Organizations (DAOs) rely on transparent, verifiable off-chain data for governance and decision-making. Oracle data can significantly influence voting, treasury management, and protocol decisions, making oracle security paramount for DAO health.

Future Trends: Decentralized Oracle Networks and Cross-Chain Interoperability

AS BLOCKCHAIN ECOSYSTEMS evolve, demand for oracle interoperability across chains grows. Cross-chain oracle services facilitate DApps interacting seamlessly across multiple blockchains, broadening their reach and utility.

Future trends involve oracle networks supporting multi-chain interoperability, enhancing the effectiveness of DeFi, NFTs, DAOs, and enterprise blockchain applications.

Conclusion

INTERACTING SECURELY with off-chain data through oracle services like Chainlink and Provable is integral to building sophisticated, reliable DApps. While these integrations provide powerful capabilities, developers must remain vigilant about security risks and implement best practices such as redundancy, thorough data validation, and decentralization. As blockchain ecosystems mature, hybrid solutions that combine decentralized oracles, off-chain computation, and sophisticated smart contracts will further unlock innovation, powering next-generation decentralized applications that bridge blockchain networks with the broader digital world.

Chapter 6: Designing the Frontend for DApps

Choosing the Right Frontend Framework

WHEN BUILDING A DECENTRALIZED Application (DApp), the frontend plays a crucial role in ensuring a seamless user experience while interacting with blockchain-based smart contracts. Selecting the right frontend framework is a critical decision that affects development speed, maintainability, and performance.

Understanding the Role of the Frontend in DApps

UNLIKE TRADITIONAL applications where the frontend interacts with a centralized backend server, DApps rely on smart contracts deployed on a blockchain. The frontend is responsible for:

- Rendering the user interface (UI) for interacting with the DApp.
- Managing user authentication through crypto wallets like MetaMask and WalletConnect.
- Sending transactions to smart contracts.
- Fetching on-chain data using Web3 libraries (such as Web3.js or Ethers.js).
- Providing a smooth and secure user experience.

Popular Frontend Frameworks for DApps

SEVERAL FRONTEND FRAMEWORKS can be used for building DApps. Below are the most popular choices:

1. React.js

REACT.JS IS THE MOST widely used frontend library for building DApps due to its component-based architecture, large ecosystem, and strong community support.

- **Pros:**

  ○ Component-based development improves code maintainability.

  ○ Large ecosystem with libraries like ethers.js and web3.js for blockchain interactions.

  ○ Strong state management options (Redux, Zustand, React Context API).

  ○ Well-supported UI frameworks such as Material-UI and Tailwind CSS.

- **Cons:**

  ○ Learning curve if unfamiliar with modern JavaScript and React concepts (hooks, functional components, etc.).

  ○ Requires additional setup for SEO (if needed) using frameworks like Next.js.

2. Vue.js

VUE.JS IS ANOTHER POPULAR frontend framework known for its simplicity and ease of integration.

- **Pros:**

  - ○ Simple and beginner-friendly compared to React.
  - ○ Smaller bundle size, making it lightweight.
  - ○ Vuex and Pinia provide easy state management.
- **Cons:**
  - ○ Smaller ecosystem compared to React.
  - ○ Less industry adoption for DApp development.

3. Angular

ANGULAR IS A FULL-FLEDGED frontend framework that enforces strong architectural patterns.

- **Pros:**
  - ○ Enterprise-grade framework with TypeScript support.
  - ○ Strong built-in features like dependency injection and form handling.
- **Cons:**
  - ○ Higher learning curve compared to React and Vue.
  - ○ Overhead due to its strict architectural patterns.

Key Considerations When Choosing a Frontend Framework

WHEN SELECTING A FRONTEND framework for a DApp, consider the following:

- **Developer Experience:** React provides the best developer experience due to its vast ecosystem and component-based architecture.

- **Performance:** Vue.js offers better performance for lightweight applications.

- **Enterprise Needs:** If working on a large-scale, enterprise-grade project, Angular might be the best choice.

- **Community Support:** React and Vue.js have strong community support, making problem-solving easier.

- **Integration with Web3:** React has better integration with blockchain libraries like Ethers.js and Web3.js.

Setting Up a DApp Frontend with React.js

BELOW IS A STEP-BY-step guide to setting up a React-based frontend for a DApp.

1. Create a New React App

TO START A NEW REACT project, use the following command:

npx create-react-app my-dapp—template typescript

cd my-dapp

2. Install Web3 Libraries

TO INTERACT WITH THE blockchain, install ethers.js:

npm install ethers

Alternatively, install web3.js:

```
npm install web3
```

3. Create a Wallet Connection Component

A REACT COMPONENT TO connect a wallet using ethers.js:

```
import { useState } from "react";

import { ethers } from "ethers";

const ConnectWallet = () => {

const [account, setAccount] = useState("");

const connectWallet = async () => {

if (window.ethereum) {

try {

const provider = new
ethers.providers.Web3Provider(window.ethereum);

await window.ethereum.request({ method: "eth_requestAccounts"
});

const signer = provider.getSigner();

const address = await signer.getAddress();

setAccount(address);

} catch (error) {

console.error("Wallet connection failed", error);
```

```
}
} else {
alert("Please install MetaMask!");
}
};
return (
<div>
{account ? <p>Connected: {account}</p> : <button onClick={connectWallet}>Connect Wallet</button>}
</div>
);
};
export default ConnectWallet;
```

4. Fetch Blockchain Data

TO RETRIEVE DATA FROM a smart contract, you need an ABI (Application Binary Interface) and a contract address.

Example of fetching data from a smart contract:

```
import { useEffect, useState } from "react";
import { ethers } from "ethers";
import contractABI from "./abi.json"; // Load ABI file
```

```
const contractAddress = "0xYourContractAddress"; // Replace with actual contract address

const FetchData = () => {

const [data, setData] = useState("");

useEffect(() => {

const fetchData = async () => {

if (window.ethereum) {

const provider = new ethers.providers.Web3Provider(window.ethereum);

const contract = new ethers.Contract(contractAddress, contractABI, provider);

try {

const value = await contract.someFunction(); // Replace with actual contract function

setData(value);

} catch (error) {

console.error("Error fetching data", error);

}

}

};

fetchData();

}, []);
```

```
return <p>Blockchain Data: {data}</p>;

};

export default FetchData;
```

Enhancing DApp Frontend with UI Libraries

FOR BETTER DESIGN, use UI libraries:

- **Material-UI:** npm install @mui/material @emotion/react @emotion/styled
- **Tailwind CSS:** npm install -D tailwindcss postcss autoprefixer

Example of using Tailwind in React:

```
const Button = () => (

<button className="bg-blue-500 text-white px-4 py-2 rounded-lg">

Click Me

</button>

);
```

Conclusion

CHOOSING THE RIGHT frontend framework for DApps is essential for ensuring a smooth user experience. React.js is the most popular choice due to its flexibility, extensive community support, and seamless integration with Web3 libraries. Setting up a frontend involves installing Web3 libraries, creating wallet connection components, fetching smart contract data, and improving UI with styling libraries like Tailwind CSS.

By following best practices and utilizing modern frontend tools, developers can create efficient, scalable, and user-friendly DApps.

Integrating Wallets and Authentication

DECENTRALIZED APPLICATIONS (DApps) rely on blockchain networks for transactions and user interactions. Unlike traditional web applications that use centralized authentication systems (such as email/password or OAuth), DApps authenticate users using cryptocurrency wallets. These wallets act as identity providers, enabling users to sign transactions and interact with smart contracts securely.

Understanding Crypto Wallets in DApps

A CRYPTO WALLET IS a software application or hardware device that allows users to store, send, and receive digital assets. In the context of DApps, wallets provide authentication and authorization mechanisms by signing transactions with private keys.

Types of Wallets

1. **Browser Extension Wallets** – Installed as browser extensions (e.g., MetaMask, Rabby).
2. **Mobile Wallets** – Mobile applications that provide access to decentralized applications (e.g., Trust Wallet, Coinbase Wallet).
3. **Hardware Wallets** – Physical devices used to store private keys securely (e.g., Ledger, Trezor).
4. **Smart Contract Wallets** – Wallets that offer additional

functionalities like multi-signature security (e.g., Argent, Gnosis Safe).

Wallet Authentication in DApps

AUTHENTICATION IN DAPPS is handled differently compared to traditional applications:

- Users authenticate by connecting their wallet to the DApp.
- Instead of passwords, authentication is done by signing a message with the wallet's private key.
- Transactions are authorized by signing them within the wallet interface.
- Web3 libraries such as **Web3.js** and **Ethers.js** enable interaction between the DApp and blockchain networks.

Integrating MetaMask for Authentication

METAMASK IS THE MOST commonly used wallet for Ethereum-based DApps. It acts as a gateway to blockchain networks, allowing users to sign transactions and authenticate securely.

1. Installing MetaMask

TO USE METAMASK, INSTALL the browser extension fromMetaMask's official website[5].

5. https://metamask.io/

2. Detecting MetaMask in a DApp

BEFORE INTERACTING with MetaMask, ensure it is installed and accessible.

```
const isMetaMaskInstalled = () => {

return typeof window.ethereum !== "undefined";

};

console.log("MetaMask Installed:", isMetaMaskInstalled());
```

If MetaMask is installed, window.ethereum will be available in the browser.

3. Connecting MetaMask to the DApp

TO AUTHENTICATE USERS, request permission to access their wallet.

```
import { useState } from "react";

const ConnectWallet = () => {

const [account, setAccount] = useState("");

const connectWallet = async () => {

if (window.ethereum) {

try {

const accounts = await window.ethereum.request({

method: "eth_requestAccounts",

});
```

```
setAccount(accounts[0]);

} catch (error) {

console.error("Wallet connection failed:", error);

}

} else {

alert("MetaMask is not installed!");

}

};

return (

<div>

{account ? <p>Connected: {account}</p> : <button onClick={connectWallet}>Connect Wallet</button>}

</div>

);

};

export default ConnectWallet;
```

- eth_requestAccounts prompts the user to connect their wallet.
- Once connected, the user's wallet address is stored in the account state.

Signing Messages for Authentication

ONCE A WALLET IS CONNECTED, it is important to verify ownership by signing a message.

```
import { ethers } from "ethers";

const signMessage = async () => {

if (!window.ethereum) {

alert("Please install MetaMask!");

return;

}

const provider = new ethers.providers.Web3Provider(window.ethereum);

const signer = provider.getSigner();

const message = "Sign this message to authenticate!";

try {

const signature = await signer.signMessage(message);

console.log("Signature:", signature);

} catch (error) {

console.error("Signing failed:", error);

}

};
```

- The user signs a message using their private key.

- The DApp verifies the signature to confirm ownership.

Verifying a Signed Message

ONCE A USER SIGNS A message, the DApp can verify the signature using ethers.js.

```
const verifySignature = async (message, signature, address) => {

const recoveredAddress = ethers.utils.verifyMessage(message, signature);

return recoveredAddress === address;

};
```

If the recovered address matches the wallet address, authentication is successful.

Using WalletConnect for Mobile Wallet Authentication

WHILE METAMASK IS WIDELY used, some users prefer mobile wallets. **WalletConnect** allows users to scan a QR code and authenticate using mobile wallets.

1. Installing WalletConnect Dependencies

```
NPM INSTALL @WALLETCONNECT/web3-provider
```

2. Connecting to WalletConnect

```
IMPORT WALLETCONNECTPROVIDER from "@walletconnect/web3-provider";

import Web3 from "web3";
```

```
const connectWalletConnect = async () => {
const provider = new WalletConnectProvider({
rpc: {
1: "https://mainnet.infura.io/v3/YOUR_INFURA_PROJECT_ID",
},
});
await provider.enable();
const web3 = new Web3(provider);
const accounts = await web3.eth.getAccounts();
console.log("Connected account:", accounts[0]);
};
```

- WalletConnect allows users to connect via QR codes.
- It supports multiple mobile wallets, including Trust Wallet and Rainbow Wallet.

Handling Network Switching

DAPPS OFTEN REQUIRE users to switch to a specific blockchain network.

Prompting Users to Switch Networks

```
CONST SWITCHNETWORK = async () => {
```

```
try {
await window.ethereum.request({
method: "wallet_switchEthereumChain",
params: [{ chainId: "0x1" }], // 0x1 = Ethereum Mainnet
});
} catch (error) {
console.error("Network switch failed:", error);
}
};
```

If the network is not available, prompt the user to add it.

```
const addNetwork = async () => {
try {
await window.ethereum.request({
method: "wallet_addEthereumChain",
params: [
{
chainId: "0x89",
chainName: "Polygon",
rpcUrls: ["https://rpc-mainnet.maticvigil.com/"],
nativeCurrency: { name: "MATIC", symbol: "MATIC", decimals: 18
},
```

```
},
],
});
} catch (error) {
console.error("Adding network failed:", error);
}
};
```

Ensuring Secure Authentication

TO ENHANCE SECURITY, follow best practices:

- **Avoid Storing Private Keys in Local Storage** – Always use secure storage solutions.
- **Use Secure Backend for Signature Verification** – Prevent replay attacks by validating nonce-based authentication.
- **Restrict Permissions** – Request only necessary permissions from the user's wallet.
- **Warn Users About Scams** – Display clear messages to educate users about signing transactions.

Conclusion

INTEGRATING WALLETS and authentication is a crucial aspect of DApp development. MetaMask is the most common solution, while WalletConnect provides an alternative for mobile wallet users. Secure authentication mechanisms, such as signed messages, ensure user identity verification without relying on centralized services. By implementing wallet authentication properly, DApps can provide a seamless and secure experience while maintaining the decentralized ethos of blockchain applications.

User Experience (UX) Considerations for Decentralized Applications

USER EXPERIENCE (UX) is a critical component of decentralized applications (DApps). While blockchain technology offers security, transparency, and decentralization, it also introduces complexities that can impact usability. Ensuring a seamless, intuitive, and engaging user experience is essential for DApp adoption.

Challenges in DApp UX

UNLIKE TRADITIONAL applications, DApps introduce unique UX challenges:

1. **Wallet Complexity** – Users must manage private keys and wallets.
2. **Transaction Delays** – Blockchain transactions require confirmations, causing delays.
3. **Gas Fees** – Users must pay gas fees, which fluctuate unpredictably.
4. **Security Concerns** – Phishing attacks and wallet scams can cause user hesitation.
5. **Network Congestion** – High traffic can slow down transactions, frustrating users.

Designing a DApp with an optimal UX requires addressing these challenges while maintaining decentralization and security.

Key UX Principles for DApps

TO IMPROVE UX IN DAPPS, developers must focus on:

- **Minimizing friction in onboarding**
- **Providing clear transaction feedback**
- **Reducing gas fee complexities**
- **Enhancing security without degrading usability**
- **Ensuring responsive and intuitive UI design**

1. Simplifying User Onboarding

TRADITIONAL APPLICATIONS use email/password authentication, while DApps rely on wallets. The onboarding experience should be as smooth as possible.

One-Click Wallet Connection

INSTEAD OF ASKING USERS to manually enter wallet addresses, provide a simple "**Connect Wallet**" button.

```
import { useState } from "react";

import { ethers } from "ethers";

const ConnectWallet = () => {

const [account, setAccount] = useState("");

const connectWallet = async () => {

if (window.ethereum) {

try {
```

```
const provider = new ethers.providers.Web3Provider(window.ethereum);

await provider.send("eth_requestAccounts", []);

const signer = provider.getSigner();

setAccount(await signer.getAddress());

} catch (error) {

console.error("Wallet connection failed:", error);

}

} else {

alert("Please install MetaMask!");

}

};

return (

<div>

{account ? <p>Connected: {account}</p> : <button onClick={connectWallet}>Connect Wallet</button>}

</div>

);

};

export default ConnectWallet;
```

UX Best Practices:

- Support multiple wallet providers (MetaMask, WalletConnect).
- Provide informative tooltips for first-time users.
- Auto-detect installed wallets and offer relevant options.

2. Improving Transaction Feedback

UNLIKE CENTRALIZED applications, blockchain transactions take time to process. Users must wait for confirmation, which can cause confusion.

Real-Time Transaction Status

A TRANSACTION GOES through multiple states:

1. **Pending** – Transaction is submitted but not confirmed.
2. **Mined** – Transaction is successfully processed on the blockchain.
3. **Failed** – Transaction was rejected or ran out of gas.

Provide real-time transaction feedback using ethers.js:

```
const sendTransaction = async () => {

if (!window.ethereum) {

alert("Wallet not detected!");

return;

}

const provider = new ethers.providers.Web3Provider(window.ethereum);
```

```
const signer = provider.getSigner();
try {
const tx = await signer.sendTransaction({
to: "0xRecipientAddress",
value: ethers.utils.parseEther("0.01"),
});
console.log("Transaction sent:", tx.hash);
const receipt = await tx.wait();
console.log("Transaction confirmed:", receipt);
} catch (error) {
console.error("Transaction failed:", error);
}
};
```

UX Best Practices:

- Show transaction progress (e.g., "Pending...", "Confirmed").
- Provide estimated wait times using historical data.
- Offer a way to view the transaction on block explorers like Etherscan.

3. Reducing Gas Fee Complexity

USERS OFTEN STRUGGLE with gas fees. Provide tools to estimate fees and allow users to adjust gas prices.

Displaying Gas Fee Estimates

```
CONST ESTIMATEGAS = async () => {

if (!window.ethereum) {

alert("Wallet not detected!");

return;

}

const provider = new ethers.providers.Web3Provider(window.ethereum);

const gasPrice = await provider.getGasPrice();

console.log("Current gas price:", ethers.utils.formatUnits(gasPrice, "gwei"), "GWEI");

};
```

UX Best Practices:

- Show real-time gas fee estimates before transaction confirmation.
- Allow users to choose between **low, medium, and high-priority** gas fees.
- Integrate with Layer 2 solutions (Polygon, Arbitrum) for lower fees.

4. Enhancing Security Without Hurting Usability

SECURITY IS ESSENTIAL, but poor UX can lead to user frustration.

Protect Users from Scam Transactions

USERS SHOULD ALWAYS know what they're signing. Provide a readable summary of transactions before approval.

Example: Instead of showing raw hexadecimal data, display:

You are sending 0.5 ETH to Address: 0x123...ABC

Enable EIP-712 for Human-Readable Signing

ETHEREUM'S **EIP-712** allows structured signing instead of raw hex data.

```
const signTypedData = async () => {

if (!window.ethereum) {

alert("Wallet not detected!");

return;

}

const provider = new ethers.providers.Web3Provider(window.ethereum);

const signer = provider.getSigner();

const message = {

domain: { name: "MyDApp", version: "1", chainId: 1 },
```

```
message: { action: "Authorize Login" },
primaryType: "Auth",
types: { Auth: [{ name: "action", type: "string" }] },
};
const signature = await signer._signTypedData(
message.domain,
message.types,
message.message
);
console.log("Signed message:", signature);
};
```

UX Best Practices:

- Always show users what they're signing.
- Warn users before sending funds or performing sensitive actions.
- Avoid requiring private key exports.

5. Creating an Intuitive and Responsive UI

DAPPS SHOULD FOLLOW modern design principles.

UI Frameworks for DApp Development

- **Material-UI:** Well-structured components with built-in accessibility.
- **Tailwind CSS:** Utility-first CSS framework for rapid styling.
- **Ant Design:** Feature-rich UI library for enterprise applications.

Example: Styling a DApp Button with Tailwind

```
CONST BUTTON = () => (

<button className="bg-blue-600 hover:bg-blue-700 text-white px-4 py-2 rounded">

Click Me

</button>

);
```

UX Best Practices:

- Use responsive design for mobile and desktop users.
- Minimize distractions and guide users through the process.
- Provide light and dark themes for better accessibility.

6. Ensuring Performance and Scalability

DAPPS MUST BE OPTIMIZED for speed, as blockchain interactions introduce latency.

Optimizing Frontend Performance

- **Lazy Load Components:** Use React.lazy() for on-demand loading.
- **Optimize API Calls:** Batch multiple blockchain queries to reduce network requests.
- **Reduce DOM Updates:** Use React's useMemo() and useCallback() to prevent unnecessary re-renders.

Using Off-Chain Data Solutions

FETCHING BLOCKCHAIN data can be slow. Use indexing solutions like **The Graph** or **Moralis** to improve performance.

```
const fetchData = async () => {

const response = await fetch("https://api.thegraph.com/subgraphs/name/protocol/example");

const data = await response.json();

console.log(data);

};
```

UX Best Practices:

- Prefetch frequently accessed data.

- Cache results to minimize redundant blockchain queries.
- Use pagination for large datasets.

Conclusion

USER EXPERIENCE IS a fundamental aspect of DApp adoption. By simplifying wallet onboarding, providing real-time transaction feedback, reducing gas fee complexities, enhancing security, designing intuitive UIs, and optimizing performance, developers can create DApps that are both **functional and user-friendly**. By focusing on UX best practices, DApps can bridge the gap between decentralization and mainstream usability.

Ensuring Performance and Scalability

DECENTRALIZED APPLICATIONS (DApps) face unique performance and scalability challenges due to their reliance on blockchain networks. Unlike traditional applications, where transactions occur on centralized servers, DApps must interact with a distributed ledger, which can introduce latency, high computational costs, and network congestion. Ensuring a responsive user experience requires optimizing both frontend and backend components.

Understanding Performance Bottlenecks in DApps

SEVERAL FACTORS CAN impact the performance and scalability of a DApp:

1. **Blockchain Latency** – Transactions require network confirmations, leading to delays.
2. **High Gas Costs** – Executing smart contracts can be

expensive, especially on networks like Ethereum.

3. **Limited Throughput** – Blockchains have finite processing capacities, causing congestion.
4. **Frontend Inefficiencies** – Unoptimized rendering and excessive API calls slow down the UI.
5. **Scalability Constraints** – As user demand grows, a DApp must efficiently handle increased traffic.

Optimizing these areas ensures a seamless experience while maintaining decentralization and security.

1. Optimizing Smart Contracts for Performance

SMART CONTRACT EFFICIENCY is crucial for reducing transaction costs and execution time.

Use Gas-Efficient Smart Contract Designs

GAS COSTS DEPEND ON computational complexity. Reduce unnecessary computations using:

- **Storage Optimization** – Minimize state variable writes, as storage is expensive.
- **Loop Efficiency** – Avoid unbounded loops that increase execution costs.
- **Event Logging** – Use events to store temporary data instead of persistent storage.

Example: Optimized Smart Contract Using Mappings

```
// Expensive: Uses an array, requiring iterations for lookups

struct User {
```

```
uint256 id;

string name;

}

User[] users;

function findUser(uint256 _id) public view returns (string memory)
{

for (uint256 i = 0; i < users.length; i++) {

if (users[i].id == _id) {

return users[i].name;

}

}

return "";

}

// Optimized: Uses a mapping for direct access

mapping(uint256 => string) userNames;

function getUser(uint256 _id) public view returns (string memory)
{

return userNames[_id];

}
```

Best Practices for Smart Contract Optimization:

- Prefer **mappings** over **arrays** for fast lookups.

- Use **constant and immutable variables** where possible to save gas.
- Batch transactions instead of executing multiple small transactions.

2. Using Layer 2 Solutions for Scalability

LAYER 2 (L2) SOLUTIONS process transactions off-chain while maintaining blockchain security.

Popular Layer 2 Scaling Solutions

1. **Polygon (MATIC)** – Uses sidechains to reduce transaction costs.
2. **Arbitrum & Optimism** – Utilize Optimistic Rollups to scale Ethereum.
3. **zkSync & StarkNet** – Use Zero-Knowledge (ZK) Rollups for efficient validation.

Example: Deploying a Smart Contract on Polygon

```
// SPDX-LICENSE-IDENTIFIER: MIT

pragma solidity ^0.8.0;

contract Layer2Optimized {

mapping(address => uint256) public balances;

function deposit() public payable {

balances[msg.sender] += msg.value;

}
```

}

To interact with Polygon, update **MetaMask** network settings:

```
{
"networkName": "Polygon Mainnet",
"rpcUrl": "https://rpc-mainnet.maticvigil.com/",
"chainId": 137,
"symbol": "MATIC",
"explorer": "https://polygonscan.com/"
}
```

Best Practices for Layer 2 Scaling:

- Guide users on switching networks using **wallet_switchEthereumChain**.
- Provide fallback options for users unfamiliar with Layer 2.
- Ensure transaction bridging is seamless between Layer 1 and Layer 2.

3. Reducing Frontend Latency

A WELL-OPTIMIZED FRONTEND improves responsiveness, even when blockchain interactions are slow.

Use Asynchronous Data Fetching

FETCHING DATA FROM blockchain nodes can be slow. Use efficient caching and asynchronous calls.

```
import { useState, useEffect } from "react";

import { ethers } from "ethers";

const provider = new ethers.providers.JsonRpcProvider("https://mainnet.infura.io/v3/YOUR_INFURA_KEY");

const fetchBalance = async (address) => {

const balance = await provider.getBalance(address);

return ethers.utils.formatEther(balance);

};

const WalletBalance = ({ address }) => {

const [balance, setBalance] = useState(null);

useEffect(() => {

fetchBalance(address).then(setBalance);

}, [address]);

return <p>Balance: {balance} ETH</p>;

};
```

Best Practices for Frontend Performance:

- Use **lazy loading** to defer loading unnecessary UI elements.
- Implement **pagination** when displaying large datasets (e.g., transaction history).
- Optimize component rendering using **React.memo()** and **useMemo()**.

4. Offloading Data to Decentralized Storage

BLOCKCHAINS ARE NOT designed for storing large amounts of data. Use **decentralized storage** solutions like:

1. **IPFS (InterPlanetary File System)** – Stores files with content-based addressing.
2. **Arweave** – Provides permanent storage for blockchain-based applications.
3. **Filecoin** – A decentralized storage network with economic incentives.

Example: Uploading Files to IPFS

```
IMPORT { CREATE } FROM "ipfs-http-client";

const ipfs = create({ url: "https://ipfs.infura.io:5001/api/v0" });

const uploadFile = async (file) => {

const added = await ipfs.add(file);

console.log("IPFS Hash:", added.path);
```

```
};
```

Best Practices for Decentralized Storage:

- Store only essential data on-chain; move bulk storage off-chain.
- Use **content hashes** for data verification.
- Provide users with clear **file retrieval options.**

5. Handling High Traffic and Load Balancing

A SCALABLE DAPP MUST efficiently handle increased user activity.

Use Blockchain Indexing Services

FETCHING DATA DIRECTLY from the blockchain can be slow. Use indexing services like:

- **The Graph** – Allows querying blockchain data using GraphQL.
- **Alchemy & Infura** – Provide high-performance blockchain RPC services.

Example: Querying Blockchain Data with The Graph

```
QUERY {
transactions(first: 10) {
id
```

```
from
to
value
}
}
```

Load Balancing with Multiple RPC Providers

IF A SINGLE RPC PROVIDER fails, your DApp should automatically switch to another provider.

```
const rpcProviders = [
"https://mainnet.infura.io/v3/YOUR_INFURA_KEY",
"https://rpc.ankr.com/eth",
"https://eth-mainnet.alchemyapi.io/v2/
YOUR_ALCHEMY_KEY"
];
const getProvider = () => {
const randomIndex = Math.floor(Math.random() *
rpcProviders.length);
return new
ethers.providers.JsonRpcProvider(rpcProviders[randomIndex]);
};
```

Best Practices for Load Handling:

- Implement **failover mechanisms** for RPC endpoints.
- Use **batch requests** to minimize blockchain calls.
- Optimize database queries when using off-chain storage.

6. Ensuring Mobile Performance and Accessibility

A GROWING NUMBER OF users interact with DApps via mobile wallets. Optimize mobile UX by:

1. **Using Mobile-Friendly UI Frameworks** – Tailwind CSS, Material-UI.
2. **Reducing JavaScript Bundle Size** – Use tree shaking to remove unused code.
3. **Optimizing Touch Interactions** – Ensure buttons and form inputs are mobile-friendly.

Example: Optimized Mobile UI with Tailwind

```
const MobileButton = () => (

<button className="bg-blue-500 text-white text-lg px-6 py-3 rounded-lg">

Connect Wallet

</button>

);
```

Conclusion

PERFORMANCE AND SCALABILITY are essential for ensuring a smooth user experience in DApps. By optimizing smart contracts, leveraging Layer 2 solutions, reducing frontend latency, utilizing decentralized storage, handling high traffic efficiently, and optimizing for mobile users, DApps can provide a **fast, secure, and scalable** experience. Implementing these best practices ensures that a DApp remains functional even as user demand and blockchain complexity grow.

Chapter 7: Advanced DApp Development and Deployment

Layer 2 Scaling Solutions (Polygon, Arbitrum, Optimism)

SCALABILITY HAS BEEN one of the most critical challenges in blockchain technology. As more users interact with decentralized applications (DApps), network congestion, slow transaction speeds, and high gas fees become major roadblocks to mainstream adoption. Layer 2 scaling solutions address these issues by enabling off-chain computations while maintaining the security of the main blockchain (Layer 1).

This section explores the different Layer 2 scaling solutions available, their mechanisms, implementation strategies, and best practices for integrating them into DApps.

Understanding Layer 2 Scaling

LAYER 2 REFERS TO SECONDARY frameworks or protocols built on top of an existing blockchain to improve scalability and transaction throughput. These solutions process transactions off-chain, reducing the load on the main chain while ensuring security and decentralization.

Key benefits of Layer 2 solutions include:

- **Lower Gas Fees**: Transactions are processed off-chain and settled in batches, significantly reducing costs.

- **Faster Transactions**: By handling transactions outside the main blockchain, Layer 2 solutions increase transaction speed.

- **Enhanced Scalability**: Offloading transactions to a secondary layer allows more users to interact with DApps without network congestion.

Common Layer 2 Solutions

SEVERAL LAYER 2 SCALING technologies have emerged to address blockchain scalability. Below, we explore some of the most widely adopted solutions:

1. State Channels

STATE CHANNELS ALLOW multiple transactions to occur off-chain between participants, only settling the final state on-chain. This reduces the number of transactions that need to be recorded on the main blockchain.

How State Channels Work:

- Two or more parties lock a portion of funds in a multi-signature smart contract.

- They conduct multiple transactions off-chain, updating the state as needed.

- When the channel is closed, the final state is submitted to the blockchain.

Example Use Case:

- Payment channels like Bitcoin's Lightning Network or Ethereum's Raiden Network enable fast microtransactions.

2. Plasma

PLASMA IS A FRAMEWORK for building scalable decentralized applications by creating child chains that operate independently but periodically commit data to the main blockchain.

Key Features of Plasma:

- Child chains handle transactions, reducing congestion on the main chain.
- Users can exit the Plasma chain and return to the main chain when needed.
- Fraud-proof mechanisms ensure security.

Example Use Case:

- Plasma is ideal for applications that require high transaction throughput, such as gaming and micro-payment solutions.

3. Rollups

ROLLUPS BUNDLE MULTIPLE transactions into a single transaction before submitting them to the main blockchain, significantly reducing gas fees and increasing scalability.

Types of Rollups:

- **Optimistic Rollups** (e.g., Optimism, Arbitrum): Assume transactions are valid unless proven otherwise via fraud proofs.

- **Zero-Knowledge (ZK) Rollups** (e.g., zkSync, StarkNet): Use cryptographic proofs to verify transactions before submitting them on-chain.

Comparison of Rollups:

Feature	Optimistic Rollups	ZK Rollups
Security Mechanism	Fraud Proofs	Validity Proofs
Finality Time	Slower (fraud-proof challenge period)	Faster (immediate verification)
Gas Cost	Lower than Layer 1 but higher than ZK	Lower than Optimistic Rollups
Best Use Cases	General-purpose DApps, DeFi	Payments, high-frequency trading

Implementing Layer 2 in a DApp

TO INTEGRATE A LAYER 2 solution into a DApp, developers typically follow these steps:

1. **Choose a Suitable Layer 2 Network**

   ○ Consider factors such as cost, speed, security, and ecosystem support.

   ○ Popular choices include **Polygon, Arbitrum, Optimism, zkSync, and StarkNet.**

2. **Deploy Smart Contracts on Layer 2**

○ Modify existing smart contracts to work on the chosen Layer 2.

○ Many Layer 2 solutions are EVM-compatible, meaning Solidity contracts can be redeployed with minimal modifications.

3. **Integrate Layer 2 SDKs and APIs**

○ Most Layer 2 networks provide developer tools for seamless integration.

○ Example: Using the ethers.js library to interact with Optimism.

```
import { ethers } from "ethers";

const provider = new ethers.providers.JsonRpcProvider("https://mainnet.optimism.io");

const signer = provider.getSigner();

const contractAddress = "0xYourContractAddress";

const contractABI = [...]; // Replace with actual ABI

const contract = new ethers.Contract(contractAddress, contractABI, signer);
```

4. **Migrate Users and Funds to Layer 2**

○ Implement bridges that allow users to transfer assets from Layer 1 to Layer 2.

○ Example: **Polygon's PoS Bridge** enables seamless asset transfers between Ethereum and Polygon.

5. **Monitor Transactions and Performance**

○ Use analytics tools to track transaction throughput, gas savings, and user experience.

○ Example: **The Graph** provides indexing and querying capabilities for blockchain data.

Best Practices for Layer 2 Adoption

TO ENSURE A SMOOTH transition to Layer 2, developers should follow these best practices:

- **Choose a Layer 2 Solution Aligned with Your Use Case**

  Not all Layer 2 solutions are suitable for every application. Select one based on your DApp's requirements (e.g., DeFi, gaming, payments).

- **Optimize Smart Contracts for Gas Efficiency**

  Even though Layer 2 reduces costs, gas optimization is still crucial to maintain affordability.

- **Implement Robust Security Measures**

  Since some Layer 2 solutions rely on fraud proofs, rigorous security audits are essential to prevent attacks.

- **Educate Users About the Transition**

  Provide clear instructions on how to bridge assets and interact with the Layer 2 network.

Conclusion

LAYER 2 SCALING SOLUTIONS are revolutionizing blockchain development by making DApps more scalable, efficient, and cost-effective. By leveraging technologies like rollups, state channels, and Plasma, developers can build high-performance applications that cater to a global user base without compromising decentralization or security.

In the next section, we will explore **cross-chain interoperability and bridges**, which allow DApps to interact across multiple blockchains seamlessly.

Cross-Chain Interoperability and Bridges

BLOCKCHAIN TECHNOLOGY has revolutionized various industries by enabling decentralized and trustless transactions. However, most blockchain networks operate in silos, making it difficult for decentralized applications (DApps) to interact across multiple chains. Cross-chain interoperability solves this issue by allowing different blockchains to communicate and exchange assets and data seamlessly. This section explores the importance of cross-chain interoperability, different types of blockchain bridges, implementation strategies, and best practices for building cross-chain DApps.

Importance of Cross-Chain Interoperability

CROSS-CHAIN INTEROPERABILITY is crucial for the growth of the decentralized ecosystem. It enhances the functionality, scalability, and user experience of DApps by allowing them to leverage multiple blockchains simultaneously. Some key benefits include:

- **Expanded Liquidity**: Users can access liquidity pools from multiple blockchains, improving capital efficiency.

- **Enhanced Scalability**: Workloads can be distributed across multiple blockchains, reducing congestion on a single network.

- **Increased Flexibility**: DApps can utilize the unique features of different blockchains, such as Ethereum's smart contracts and Binance Smart Chain's low transaction fees.

- **Seamless Asset Transfers**: Users can move assets between blockchains without relying on centralized exchanges.

Types of Cross-Chain Bridges

BLOCKCHAIN BRIDGES facilitate interoperability by enabling asset transfers and data exchange between different networks. Below are the main types of blockchain bridges:

1. Trusted Bridges

TRUSTED BRIDGES RELY on a centralized entity or group of validators to facilitate cross-chain transactions. Users deposit assets into a smart contract, and an equivalent amount is minted on the destination chain.

Pros:

- High-speed transactions

- User-friendly experience

Cons:

- Centralization risk
- Vulnerable to security breaches

Example: Binance Bridge allows users to convert tokens between Ethereum and Binance Smart Chain.

2. Trustless Bridges

TRUSTLESS BRIDGES USE smart contracts and cryptographic mechanisms to enable decentralized asset transfers. These bridges do not rely on intermediaries, ensuring greater security.

Pros:

- Fully decentralized
- Transparent and secure

Cons:

- Complex implementation
- Higher computational costs

Example: Wormhole, a decentralized bridge supporting multiple blockchains.

3. Federated Bridges

FEDERATED BRIDGES ARE operated by a consortium of entities that collectively validate cross-chain transactions. These bridges are commonly used by enterprise blockchain networks.

Pros:

- Improved security through consortium governance
- Suitable for permissioned blockchains

Cons:

- Partial centralization
- Slower transaction speeds

Example: RSK Bridge connects Bitcoin with Ethereum-compatible smart contracts.

How Cross-Chain Bridges Work

CROSS-CHAIN BRIDGES function through a series of steps that ensure secure asset transfers between blockchains:

1. **Locking Assets on Source Chain**
   The user sends tokens to a smart contract on the source blockchain, where they are locked as collateral.
2. **Verification by Validators or Smart Contracts**
   A set of validators or a smart contract verifies the transaction and confirms the asset transfer request.
3. **Minting Wrapped Tokens on the Destination Chain**
   An equivalent amount of wrapped tokens is created on the destination blockchain, maintaining a 1:1 peg with the locked assets.
4. **Redeeming Tokens Back to Source Chain**
   When the user wants to retrieve the original assets, the wrapped tokens are burned on the destination chain, and the locked assets are released on the source chain.

Implementing Cross-Chain Bridges in DApps

DEVELOPERS CAN INTEGRATE cross-chain functionality into their DApps using blockchain bridge protocols and interoperability frameworks. Below are the key steps for building a cross-chain DApp:

1. Choose a Cross-Chain Protocol

SEVERAL CROSS-CHAIN protocols provide pre-built solutions for interoperability. Some popular options include:

- **Polkadot**: Uses a relay chain to connect different blockchains.
- **Cosmos**: Implements the Inter-Blockchain Communication (IBC) protocol.
- **Thorchain**: Enables native asset swaps across multiple blockchains.

2. Develop Smart Contracts for Asset Bridging

TO BRIDGE ASSETS, DEVELOPERS need to create smart contracts that handle token locking, minting, and burning.

Example Solidity contract for asset locking:

```
pragma solidity ^0.8.0;

contract CrossChainBridge {

mapping(address => uint256) public lockedFunds;

event Locked(address indexed user, uint256 amount);
```

```
event Released(address indexed user, uint256 amount);

function lockFunds() external payable {

require(msg.value > 0, "Amount must be greater than zero");

lockedFunds[msg.sender] += msg.value;

emit Locked(msg.sender, msg.value);

}

function releaseFunds(address payable user, uint256 amount) external {

require(lockedFunds[user] >= amount, "Insufficient funds");

lockedFunds[user] -= amount;

user.transfer(amount);

emit Released(user, amount);

}

}
```

3. Integrate Off-Chain Oracles for Cross-Chain Validation

TO ENSURE SECURE CROSS-chain transactions, DApps can use oracles like Chainlink or Band Protocol to verify transactions.

```
import { ethers } from "ethers";

const provider = new ethers.providers.JsonRpcProvider("https://polygon-rpc.com/");
```

```
const oracleContract = new ethers.Contract(oracleAddress, oracleABI, provider);

async function verifyTransaction(txHash) {

const isValid = await oracleContract.validateTransaction(txHash);

return isValid;

}
```

4. Enable Multi-Chain User Experience

DAPPS SHOULD PROVIDE users with seamless access to multiple blockchains by integrating wallet providers like MetaMask, WalletConnect, and RainbowKit.

Example UI integration:

```
import Web3 from "web3";

const web3 = new Web3(window.ethereum);

await window.ethereum.request({ method: "eth_requestAccounts" });

const chainId = await web3.eth.getChainId();

if (chainId !== expectedChainId) {

alert("Please switch to the correct blockchain network.");

}
```

Challenges in Cross-Chain Interoperability

WHILE CROSS-CHAIN INTEROPERABILITY provides numerous benefits, it also presents several challenges:

- **Security Risks**: Bridges are often targeted by hackers due to vulnerabilities in smart contracts and validation mechanisms.

- **Complexity**: Implementing cross-chain transactions requires additional development efforts and coordination across multiple protocols.

- **Liquidity Fragmentation**: Assets spread across multiple chains may lead to reduced liquidity in decentralized finance (DeFi) applications.

Best Practices for Cross-Chain DApp Development

TO BUILD SECURE AND efficient cross-chain DApps, developers should follow these best practices:

- **Use Audited Bridges**: Choose well-audited and battle-tested bridges to minimize security risks.

- **Implement Robust Smart Contract Security**: Conduct thorough testing and use formal verification tools to identify vulnerabilities.

- **Monitor Network Congestion**: Optimize gas fees and transaction batching to reduce costs.

- **Enhance User Experience**: Provide clear instructions for users on how to bridge assets safely.

Conclusion

CROSS-CHAIN INTEROPERABILITY is a critical component of the future blockchain ecosystem, enabling seamless communication and asset transfers between multiple networks. By leveraging blockchain bridges, smart contracts, oracles, and interoperability protocols, developers can create powerful and scalable DApps that provide users with a unified experience across different blockchains.

In the next section, we will explore **Governance and Decentralized Autonomous Organizations (DAOs)**, which play a crucial role in the decision-making processes of decentralized applications.

Governance and Decentralized Autonomous Organizations (DAOs)

GOVERNANCE IS A FUNDAMENTAL aspect of decentralized applications (DApps) and blockchain ecosystems. Traditional organizations rely on centralized decision-making, where a board of directors or executives dictate policies. In contrast, blockchain-based governance models utilize Decentralized Autonomous Organizations (DAOs) to enable community-driven decision-making.

This section explores the concept of DAOs, their benefits, governance mechanisms, implementation strategies, and best practices for integrating DAO governance into DApps.

Understanding Decentralized Autonomous Organizations (DAOs)

A **Decentralized Autonomous Organization (DAO)** is a blockchain-based entity that operates without centralized control.

It uses smart contracts to automate decision-making processes, ensuring transparency and eliminating the need for intermediaries.

Key Characteristics of DAOs:

- **Decentralization**: Governance decisions are made collectively by token holders.

- **Transparency**: Smart contracts execute predefined rules on-chain, visible to all participants.

- **Autonomy**: DAOs function independently of traditional management structures.

- **Community Participation**: Token holders propose and vote on changes to the protocol.

Examples of DAOs in Action:

- **MakerDAO**: Governs the DAI stablecoin through community voting.

- **Uniswap DAO**: Allows users to vote on protocol upgrades and fee structures.

- **Aragon**: Provides a framework for creating and managing DAOs.

DAO Governance Models

DIFFERENT DAOS IMPLEMENT various governance models based on their objectives and level of decentralization. Below are the most common governance structures:

1. Token-Based Governance

TOKEN-BASED GOVERNANCE grants voting rights to users based on the number of governance tokens they hold. This model is widely used in DeFi protocols and blockchain projects.

How It Works:

- Users acquire governance tokens by purchasing, staking, or contributing to the ecosystem.
- Each token represents a vote, allowing holders to influence protocol decisions.
- Proposals with majority approval are executed via smart contracts.

Example:

- **Uniswap Governance Token (UNI)**: Holders vote on protocol fee structures and treasury management.

2. Quadratic Voting

QUADRATIC VOTING IS a more democratic governance model where users allocate votes based on their level of conviction. Instead of one token equaling one vote, voting power follows a quadratic cost function.

Benefits of Quadratic Voting:

- Prevents large holders from dominating governance.
- Encourages diverse community participation.

- Reduces the risk of governance attacks by whales.

Example of Quadratic Voting Calculation: If a user wants to cast multiple votes, the cost follows this formula:

Cost=(Votes)2Cost = (Votes)^2Cost=(Votes)2

Votes Cast	Tokens Required
1	1
2	4
3	9
4	16

3. Reputation-Based Governance

SOME DAOS ASSIGN VOTING power based on reputation rather than token holdings. This model rewards active contributors rather than wealthy investors.

Features of Reputation-Based Governance:

- Users earn governance rights through contributions, development, or participation.

- Voting power is non-transferable, preventing buying influence.

- Reduces the centralization of voting power in the hands of wealthy individuals.

Example:

- **Gitcoin DAO** uses reputation-based governance to fund open-source development projects.

Implementing a DAO for DApp Governance

DEVELOPERS CAN INTEGRATE DAO governance into their DApps using smart contracts and DAO frameworks. Below is a step-by-step guide to creating a basic DAO.

Step 1: Define Governance Parameters

BEFORE CODING THE DAO, define key parameters:

- **Proposal Mechanism**: Who can submit governance proposals?
- **Voting System**: Token-based, quadratic, or reputation-based?
- **Execution Rules**: What happens after a successful vote?

Step 2: Deploy a DAO Smart Contract

THE CORE OF A DAO IS a smart contract that manages voting, proposals, and fund allocation. Below is a basic Solidity implementation of a DAO contract:

```
pragma solidity ^0.8.0;

contract DAO {

struct Proposal {

string description;

uint256 votes;

address proposer;
```

```
bool executed;

}

Proposal[] public proposals;

mapping(address => uint256) public tokenBalance;

address public owner;

event ProposalCreated(uint256 proposalId, string description, address proposer);

event Voted(uint256 proposalId, address voter);

event Executed(uint256 proposalId);

modifier onlyOwner() {

require(msg.sender == owner, "Not authorized");

_;

}

constructor() {

owner = msg.sender;

}

function createProposal(string memory _description) public {

proposals.push(Proposal(_description, 0, msg.sender, false));

emit ProposalCreated(proposals.length - 1, _description, msg.sender);

}
```

```
function vote(uint256 _proposalId) public {

require(tokenBalance[msg.sender] > 0, "No voting power");

proposals[_proposalId].votes += tokenBalance[msg.sender];

emit Voted(_proposalId, msg.sender);

}

function executeProposal(uint256 _proposalId) public onlyOwner
{

require(!proposals[_proposalId].executed, "Already executed");

require(proposals[_proposalId].votes > 100, "Not enough votes");

proposals[_proposalId].executed = true;

emit Executed(_proposalId);

}

}
```

Step 3: Integrate Governance UI

ONCE THE DAO CONTRACT is deployed, create a front-end interface for users to participate in governance.

Example UI snippet using Web3.js:

```
async function createProposal(description) {

const contract = new web3.eth.Contract(DAO_ABI,
DAO_ADDRESS);
```

```
await contract.methods.createProposal(description).send({ from: userAddress });

}

async function vote(proposalId) {

const contract = new web3.eth.Contract(DAO_ABI, DAO_ADDRESS);

await contract.methods.vote(proposalId).send({ from: userAddress });

}
```

Step 4: Enable Community Participation

ENCOURAGE ACTIVE GOVERNANCE by:

- **Providing Incentives**: Reward participants with governance tokens.
- **Conducting Regular Proposals**: Maintain engagement through consistent decision-making.
- **Ensuring Transparency**: Make voting results publicly accessible on-chain.

Challenges in DAO Governance

WHILE DAOS ENHANCE decentralization, they also face several challenges:

- **Voter Apathy**: Many token holders do not participate in governance, leading to low voter turnout.

- **Governance Attacks**: Whales or malicious actors can manipulate voting outcomes.
- **Smart Contract Risks**: Bugs in governance contracts can lead to fund losses or exploitations.
- **Legal Uncertainty**: Regulatory frameworks for DAOs remain unclear in many jurisdictions.

Best Practices for DAO Governance

TO BUILD A ROBUST AND effective DAO, developers should follow these best practices:

1. **Optimize Voting Mechanisms**: Choose the most suitable governance model based on community needs.
2. **Implement Security Audits**: Conduct third-party audits of governance contracts to prevent vulnerabilities.
3. **Encourage Community Involvement**: Use incentives and education to increase voter participation.
4. **Establish a Dispute Resolution System**: Implement safeguards against governance attacks or protocol failures.
5. **Ensure Regulatory Compliance**: Adhere to legal requirements in relevant jurisdictions.

Conclusion

DECENTRALIZED AUTONOMOUS Organizations (DAOs) are revolutionizing governance in blockchain ecosystems by enabling transparent, community-driven decision-making. By leveraging token-based voting, quadratic mechanisms, or reputation-based governance, DAOs provide a fair and democratic approach to managing decentralized projects.

In the next section, we will explore **Deploying DApps on Mainnet and Managing Updates**, where we will discuss best practices for launching a decentralized application and ensuring its ongoing maintenance.

Deploying DApps on Mainnet and Managing Updates

DEPLOYING A DECENTRALIZED application (DApp) to the mainnet is a critical milestone in its lifecycle. Unlike traditional applications, where updates and patches can be pushed at will, smart contract-based applications require careful planning to ensure a seamless and secure deployment. Additionally, once deployed, smart contracts are immutable, meaning updates require special strategies such as upgradeable contracts or proxy patterns.

This section explores the entire deployment process, from pre-launch testing and deployment best practices to managing updates and ensuring long-term maintainability.

Preparing for Mainnet Deployment

BEFORE DEPLOYING A DApp to the mainnet, thorough testing and validation are necessary to prevent security vulnerabilities, high gas costs, and inefficiencies. Below are the key steps to prepare for deployment:

1. Smart Contract Audit and Security Testing

SECURITY VULNERABILITIES in smart contracts can lead to exploits, loss of funds, and irreparable damage to the project's reputation. The following security measures should be taken:

- **Static Analysis**: Use tools like Slither, MythX, and Oyente to analyze smart contracts for vulnerabilities.

- **Unit Testing**: Write comprehensive test cases using frameworks like Hardhat, Truffle, or Foundry.

- **Gas Optimization**: Identify inefficiencies in contract execution to minimize gas costs.

- **Formal Verification**: Ensure correctness using tools like Certora or Securify.

- **Third-Party Audit**: Engage security firms such as OpenZeppelin, Trail of Bits, or ConsenSys Diligence for an independent audit.

Example Hardhat test for verifying token transfers:

```
const { expect } = require("chai");

describe("Token Contract", function () {

it("Should transfer tokens successfully", async function () {

const [owner, addr1] = await ethers.getSigners();

const Token = await ethers.getContractFactory("MyToken");

const token = await Token.deploy();

await token.deployed();

await token.transfer(addr1.address, 100);

expect(await token.balanceOf(addr1.address)).to.equal(100);

});
```

```
});
```

2. Deploying to Testnets

DEPLOYING TO ETHEREUM testnets (such as Goerli, Sepolia, or Holesky) or Layer 2 testnets (Optimism, Arbitrum, Polygon Mumbai) ensures contracts function correctly in a live but risk-free environment.

Example deployment script using Hardhat:

```
async function main() {

const [deployer] = await ethers.getSigners();

console.log("Deploying contracts with the account:", deployer.address);

const MyContract = await ethers.getContractFactory("MyContract");

const contract = await MyContract.deploy();

console.log("Contract deployed to:", contract.address);

}

main().catch((error) => {

console.error(error);

process.exit(1);

});
```

3. Setting Up a Deployment Pipeline

AUTOMATING DEPLOYMENTS using CI/CD tools ensures consistency and reduces human errors. Common tools include:

- **GitHub Actions**: Automates contract compilation, testing, and deployment.
- **Foundry**: Enables fast and efficient smart contract development.
- **Terraform & Ansible**: Manages blockchain nodes and infrastructure.

Example GitHub Actions workflow for Hardhat deployments:

```
name: Deploy Smart Contracts

on:

push:

branches:

- main

jobs:

deploy:

runs-on: ubuntu-latest

steps:

- name: Checkout Repository

uses: actions/checkout@v2
```

```
- name: Setup Node.js
uses: actions/setup-node@v2
with:
node-version: "16"
- name: Install Dependencies
run: npm install
- name: Deploy to Ethereum
run: npx hardhat run scripts/deploy.js—network mainnet
```

Deploying to Mainnet

ONCE THE SMART CONTRACT is thoroughly tested on testnets, the deployment process can proceed on the mainnet. The following steps should be followed:

1. Selecting the Right Blockchain

CHOOSING THE RIGHT blockchain or Layer 2 network impacts transaction costs, scalability, and security. Options include:

- **Ethereum Mainnet**: High security but expensive gas fees.
- **Layer 2 Solutions (Polygon, Arbitrum, Optimism)**: Lower costs with fast transaction speeds.
- **Alternative L1s (Avalanche, BNB Chain, Solana)**: Specific use cases depending on ecosystem compatibility.

2. Funding Deployment Wallet

DEPLOYING CONTRACTS requires ETH or native tokens for gas fees. Use a dedicated deployment wallet with a multisig or hardware security.

3. Deploying with Verified Contracts

PUBLISHING CONTRACT source code on block explorers like **Etherscan, BscScan, or Polygonscan** increases transparency.

Example Hardhat command to verify a contract:

npx hardhat verify—network mainnet <contract_address>

4. Post-Deployment Security Checks

- **Check Contract Ownership**: Ensure deployer wallet has limited permissions.
- **Enable Timelocks for Governance**: Prevent admin abuse.
- **Monitor Contract Activity**: Use tools like Tenderly or OpenZeppelin Defender.

Managing DApp Updates

SMART CONTRACTS ARE immutable once deployed, meaning updates require specific mechanisms. Below are key strategies for managing updates:

1. Upgradeable Smart Contracts

USING **proxy patterns**, developers can modify contract logic without changing storage states.

Transparent Proxy Pattern:

Uses an implementation contract behind a proxy contract. Users interact with the proxy, while the implementation logic can be upgraded.

Example upgradeable contract using OpenZeppelin:

```
// SPDX-License-Identifier: MIT

pragma solidity ^0.8.0;

import "@openzeppelin/contracts/proxy/TransparentUpgradeableProxy.sol";

contract MyUpgradeableContract {

uint256 public version;

function setVersion(uint256 _version) public {

version = _version;

}

}
```

2. Implementing Governance-Controlled Updates

DAOS OR GOVERNANCE models can control contract upgrades to prevent centralized changes.

Example Governor contract for upgrade approval:

```
contract Governance {
address public admin;
mapping(uint256 => bool) public approvedUpgrades;
function approveUpgrade(uint256 upgradeId) external {
require(msg.sender == admin, "Only admin can approve");
approvedUpgrades[upgradeId] = true;
}
}
```

3. Using Layer 2 and Sidechains for Flexibility

- Deploy new contract versions on **Layer 2** instead of mainnet.
- Use **bridges** for asset transfers between old and new versions.

4. Implementing Feature Flags

FEATURE FLAGS ALLOW enabling/disabling new features without deploying new contracts.

Example using storage variables:

```
contract FeatureFlags {
bool public newFeatureEnabled = false;
```

```
function toggleFeature(bool _enabled) external {
newFeatureEnabled = _enabled;
}
function useFeature() external view returns (string memory) {
require(newFeatureEnabled, "Feature disabled");
return "New Feature Active";
}
}
```

Monitoring and Maintenance

DAPP DEVELOPERS MUST ensure ongoing security and performance post-deployment.

1. On-Chain Analytics

- **Dune Analytics**: Query blockchain data for user activity.
- **The Graph**: Index and fetch blockchain data efficiently.

2. Security Monitoring

- **OpenZeppelin Defender**: Real-time security monitoring for smart contracts.
- **Chainalysis & Forta**: Detects suspicious contract activity.

3. Handling Contract Exploits

IF AN EXPLOIT OCCURS:

1. **Pause Contract (if supported)**: Use OpenZeppelin's Pausable contract feature.
2. **Execute Emergency Governance Vote**: Community-driven mitigation.
3. **Communicate with Users**: Transparency is key to maintaining trust.

Example implementation of a pausable contract:

```
contract PausableContract is Ownable {
bool public paused = false;
modifier notPaused() {
require(!paused, "Contract is paused");
_;
}
function setPaused(bool _paused) external onlyOwner {
paused = _paused;
}
}
```

Conclusion

DEPLOYING A DAPP ON mainnet requires rigorous testing, security precautions, and deployment strategies to ensure success.

Managing updates in an immutable blockchain environment necessitates upgradeable contracts, governance-controlled changes, and feature flags. Additionally, continuous monitoring and maintenance are crucial for security and user trust.

In the next chapter, we will explore **Security and Best Practices for DApp Development**, detailing common vulnerabilities, auditing techniques, and strategies to build secure smart contracts.

Chapter 8: Security and Best Practices for DApp Development

Common Vulnerabilities in Smart Contracts

SECURITY IS ONE OF the most critical aspects of decentralized application (DApp) development. Due to the immutable nature of smart contracts, any vulnerability or exploit can lead to irreversible consequences, including financial losses and compromised user data. In this section, we will explore common vulnerabilities in smart contracts, their impact, and mitigation strategies.

Reentrancy Attacks

ONE OF THE MOST WELL-known vulnerabilities in Ethereum smart contracts is the **reentrancy attack**, which was famously exploited in The DAO hack of 2016. This vulnerability occurs when a contract makes an external call to another contract before updating its own state, allowing the called contract to recursively call the original contract before the first function execution completes.

Example of a Vulnerable Smart Contract

HERE'S AN EXAMPLE OF a smart contract vulnerable to a reentrancy attack:

```
// Vulnerable smart contract

pragma solidity ^0.8.0;

contract VulnerableBank {

mapping(address => uint) public balances;
```

```
function deposit() public payable {

balances[msg.sender] += msg.value;

}

function withdraw(uint _amount) public {

require(balances[msg.sender] >= _amount, "Insufficient funds");

(bool sent, ) = msg.sender.call{value: _amount}(""); // External call

require(sent, "Transfer failed");

balances[msg.sender] -= _amount; // State update happens AFTER the call

}

}
```

Attack Explanation

A MALICIOUS CONTRACT could exploit this by repeatedly calling the withdraw function before the balance is updated, draining the funds from the contract.

Mitigation Strategies

TO PREVENT REENTRANCY attacks:

1. **Use the Checks-Effects-Interactions Pattern:** Always update the contract's state before making external calls.
2. **Use ReentrancyGuard:** The OpenZeppelin ReentrancyGuard modifier prevents reentrant calls.
3. **Use transfer or send instead of call:** These functions limit

the amount of gas sent, preventing malicious contract execution.

Here's a secure implementation:

```
pragma solidity ^0.8.0;

import "@openzeppelin/contracts/security/ReentrancyGuard.sol";

contract SecureBank is ReentrancyGuard {

mapping(address => uint) public balances;

function deposit() public payable {

balances[msg.sender] += msg.value;

}

function withdraw(uint _amount) public nonReentrant {

require(balances[msg.sender] >= _amount, "Insufficient funds");

balances[msg.sender] -= _amount; // State update BEFORE the call

payable(msg.sender).transfer(_amount);

}

}
```

Front-Running Attacks

FRONT-RUNNING OCCURS when a malicious actor observes a pending transaction in the mempool and submits a transaction with a higher gas fee to get it executed first. This is particularly problematic in **Decentralized Finance (DeFi)** applications, where attackers can exploit price changes before legitimate transactions are processed.

Example of a Vulnerable Function

CONSIDER A SMART CONTRACT that allows users to bid on an auction:

```
pragma solidity ^0.8.0;

contract VulnerableAuction {

address public highestBidder;

uint public highestBid;

function bid() public payable {

require(msg.value > highestBid, "Bid too low");

highestBidder = msg.sender;

highestBid = msg.value;

}

}
```

An attacker monitoring the blockchain can quickly submit a higher bid just before a legitimate transaction is confirmed.

Mitigation Strategies

1. **Use Commit-Reveal Schemes:** Instead of sending bids directly, users first submit a **commitment** (hashed bid) and later reveal their actual bid.

2. **Use Random Delays:** Introduce unpredictable delays in processing transactions to make front-running harder.
3. **Use Private Mempools:** Some blockchain networks allow private transactions that are not visible to the public mempool.

HERE'S A SECURE COMMIT-reveal implementation:

```
pragma solidity ^0.8.0;

contract SecureAuction {

struct Bid {

bytes32 commitment;

uint revealTime;

}

mapping(address => Bid) public bids;

function commitBid(bytes32 _commitment) public {

bids[msg.sender] = Bid(_commitment, block.timestamp + 1 days);

}

function revealBid(uint _amount, bytes32 _salt) public {

require(block.timestamp >= bids[msg.sender].revealTime, "Too early to reveal");

require(keccak256(abi.encodePacked(_amount, _salt)) == bids[msg.sender].commitment, "Invalid bid");

// Process bid securely
```

```
}

}
```

Integer Overflow and Underflow

BEFORE SOLIDITY 0.8.0, integer overflows and underflows were a major security concern. If a contract did not handle arithmetic properly, an attacker could exploit integer wraparounds.

Example of Overflow

```
PRAGMA SOLIDITY ^0.6.0;

contract OverflowExample {

uint8 public count = 255;

function increment() public {

count += 1; // Wraps back to 0

}

}
```

Mitigation Strategies

1. **Use SafeMath:** The SafeMath library from OpenZeppelin prevents overflows.
2. **Upgrade to Solidity 0.8.0+:** Solidity 0.8.0 introduced built-in overflow protection.

```
PRAGMA SOLIDITY ^0.8.0;

contract SafeCounter {
```

```
uint8 public count = 255;

function increment() public {

count += 1; // Throws error instead of wrapping

}

}
```

Phishing and Social Engineering

EVEN WITH PERFECT SMART contract security, **users remain the weakest link.** Attackers often use phishing websites or malicious DApps to trick users into signing malicious transactions.

Mitigation Strategies

1. **Educate Users:** Regularly educate users on verifying smart contract addresses.
2. **Use ENS (Ethereum Name Service):** ENS domains help users verify official contracts.
3. **Implement Transaction Signing Warnings:** DApps should clearly display what users are signing before confirming transactions.

Conclusion

SECURITY IN SMART CONTRACT development is an ongoing process that requires **continuous monitoring, testing, and improvement**. By implementing best practices such as **reentrancy protection, front-running mitigations, integer safety, and user security awareness**, developers can build **resilient** and **trustworthy** DApps.

To further enhance security, smart contract developers should:

- Conduct **regular audits** with security firms.
- Use **bug bounties** to find vulnerabilities.
- Stay updated with the latest **blockchain security trends**.

By prioritizing security from the **design phase**, developers can **prevent exploits** that could lead to catastrophic losses.

Security Audits and Testing Strategies

SECURITY AUDITS AND testing are essential components of decentralized application (DApp) development. Unlike traditional applications, smart contracts are immutable once deployed, meaning that vulnerabilities cannot be patched easily. A single security flaw can lead to significant financial losses or data breaches. Therefore, implementing a robust auditing and testing strategy is critical before launching a DApp on the blockchain.

This section covers the importance of security audits, different types of audits, manual and automated testing strategies, and best practices for ensuring a secure smart contract deployment.

Importance of Security Audits in DApp Development

SECURITY AUDITS ARE necessary to:

- Identify vulnerabilities in smart contracts before deployment.

- Prevent financial losses due to exploits such as reentrancy, integer overflows, and front-running.
- Ensure compliance with industry best practices and standards.
- Build trust among users and investors.
- Reduce the attack surface by proactively fixing vulnerabilities.

By performing thorough audits, developers can mitigate security risks and enhance the robustness of their DApps.

Types of Security Audits

SECURITY AUDITS CAN be categorized into **manual audits** and **automated audits**. A comprehensive security strategy involves both.

1. Manual Audits

MANUAL SECURITY AUDITS involve **code review, logic verification, and adversarial testing** performed by security experts. Auditors analyze smart contracts for:

- Logical errors
- Business logic vulnerabilities
- Gas inefficiencies
- Compliance with best practices

Manual Audit Process

1. **Code Review:** Security experts manually inspect the Solidity code to detect vulnerabilities.
2. **Threat Modeling:** Identify potential attack vectors and assess risk exposure.
3. **Business Logic Validation:** Verify whether the smart contract functions as intended without security flaws.
4. **Edge Case Analysis:** Test the contract under extreme conditions.
5. **Mitigation Strategies:** Provide recommendations to fix vulnerabilities before deployment.

MANUAL AUDITS PROVIDE deep insights into vulnerabilities that automated tools may miss. However, they can be time-consuming and costly.

2. Automated Audits

AUTOMATED AUDITS USE security tools to analyze smart contracts for known vulnerabilities. These tools scan codebases, detect security flaws, and suggest fixes.

Popular Automated Security Audit Tools:

- **Slither:** A static analysis tool by Trail of Bits that detects vulnerabilities in Solidity smart contracts.

- **MythX:** A cloud-based security analysis platform that uses symbolic execution and fuzz testing.

- **Oyente:** A tool that analyzes smart contract execution paths to detect vulnerabilities like reentrancy and integer overflows.

- **Securify:** Developed by ETH Zurich, it performs security analysis by checking compliance with best practices.

- **SmartCheck:** A static analysis tool that identifies security issues and provides fixes.

Example: Using Slither for Automated Security Analysis

SLITHER IS A POPULAR tool for static analysis of Solidity smart contracts. To use Slither, install it via Python:

pip install slither-analyzer

Then, run a security scan on a Solidity contract:

slither contracts/MyContract.sol

The output provides a report detailing potential vulnerabilities and best practice violations.

While automated tools are fast and effective in detecting known vulnerabilities, they cannot replace manual audits, as they may generate false positives or miss logic-based flaws.

Smart Contract Testing Strategies

TESTING IS CRUCIAL to prevent security issues and ensure the expected functionality of a smart contract. There are different types of tests that developers should incorporate into their workflow.

1. Unit Testing

UNIT TESTS FOCUS ON testing individual functions in a smart contract. These tests verify that each function behaves as expected under various conditions.

Example: Writing Unit Tests with Hardhat

HARDHAT IS A WIDELY used development framework for testing smart contracts. Below is an example of a simple unit test:

```
const { expect } = require("chai");

describe("Token Contract", function () {

let Token;

let token;

let owner;

let addr1;

beforeEach(async function () {

Token = await ethers.getContractFactory("Token");

[owner, addr1] = await ethers.getSigners();

token = await Token.deploy();

});

it("Should assign total supply to owner", async function () {

const ownerBalance = await token.balanceOf(owner.address);
```

```
expect(await token.totalSupply()).to.equal(ownerBalance);

});

it("Should transfer tokens between accounts", async function () {

await token.transfer(addr1.address, 50);

expect(await token.balanceOf(addr1.address)).to.equal(50);

});

});
```

Unit tests ensure that functions work as expected, handling edge cases and invalid inputs.

2. Integration Testing

INTEGRATION TESTS VERIFY that different parts of a DApp work together correctly. This includes interactions between:

- Smart contracts
- Backend services
- Frontend applications
- Wallet integrations (e.g., MetaMask)

Example: Testing Smart Contract Interaction with Ethers.js

```
CONST { ETHERS } = require("ethers");

async function main() {
```

```
const provider = new ethers.providers.JsonRpcProvider("http://localhost:8545");

const signer = provider.getSigner();

const contract = new ethers.Contract(contractAddress, contractABI, signer);

// Call a contract function

const response = await contract.someFunction();

console.log("Response:", response);

}

main();
```

Integration tests ensure that smart contracts interact correctly with external components.

3. Fuzz Testing

FUZZ TESTING INVOLVES supplying random or unexpected inputs to a smart contract to detect vulnerabilities.

Example: Using Echidna for Fuzz Testing

```
DOCKER RUN -IT—RM TRAILOFBITS/echidna echidna-test contracts/MyContract.sol
```

Fuzz testing is useful for uncovering security issues that arise from unexpected inputs.

4. End-to-End (E2E) Testing

END-TO-END TESTS VERIFY that a complete DApp, including smart contracts, frontend, and backend, works as expected.

Example: Writing an E2E Test with Cypress

CYPRESS IS A JAVASCRIPT testing framework used for frontend testing.

```
describe("DApp Workflow", () => {

it("Allows a user to connect a wallet and execute a transaction", () =>
{

cy.visit("http://localhost:3000");

cy.get("#connectWallet").click();

cy.get("#sendTransaction").click();

cy.get("#confirmationMessage").should("contain",          "Transaction
successful");

});

});
```

E2E tests simulate user interactions and ensure that all components function properly together.

Best Practices for Secure Smart Contract Development

1. **Use Established Libraries**
   Instead of writing custom implementations, leverage well-

audited libraries like OpenZeppelin.

2. **Apply the Principle of Least Privilege**
   Grant minimal permissions to contracts and users to reduce the attack surface.
3. **Implement Circuit Breakers**
   Add emergency stop mechanisms to halt contract execution in case of an exploit.
4. **Perform Code Reviews and Peer Audits**
   Having multiple security experts review your code helps identify vulnerabilities.
5. **Conduct Regular Security Audits**
   Engage third-party security firms to audit your smart contracts before deployment.
6. **Use Multi-Signature Wallets for Administration**
   Deploy administrative functions under a multi-signature setup to prevent unauthorized changes.
7. **Monitor Deployed Contracts**
   Set up on-chain monitoring and alerts to detect unusual contract interactions.

Conclusion

SECURITY AUDITS AND thorough testing are critical for ensuring that smart contracts function securely and reliably. By combining **manual audits, automated tools, and rigorous testing**, developers can significantly reduce the risk of vulnerabilities.

A secure DApp is **not just about coding best practices but also about maintaining a proactive security strategy** throughout its lifecycle. Regular updates, security monitoring, and community involvement further enhance the security and trustworthiness of decentralized applications.

Best Practices for Private Key Management and User Security

SECURITY IN DECENTRALIZED applications (DApps) extends beyond smart contract vulnerabilities and auditing. One of the most crucial aspects of DApp security is **private key management and user security**. Poor key management can lead to loss of assets, identity theft, and unauthorized access.

This section explores the risks associated with private key mismanagement, best practices for securing private keys, and strategies to enhance user security in DApps.

Understanding Private Key Security Risks

PRIVATE KEYS ACT AS the **sole access point** for controlling blockchain accounts. Unlike traditional applications, where lost passwords can be recovered, blockchain transactions are **immutable**, and key loss results in **permanent account lockout**.

Common security threats include:

1. **Phishing Attacks** – Malicious websites trick users into revealing private keys or signing malicious transactions.
2. **Key Leakage** – Storing private keys in exposed locations, such as code repositories or local files, can lead to theft.
3. **Malware and Keyloggers** – Malware can steal private keys from browsers, wallets, or clipboard history.
4. **Man-in-the-Middle (MitM) Attacks** – Attackers intercept data transmitted between users and blockchain nodes.
5. **Improper Key Backup Practices** – If users do not securely back up their private keys, accidental loss can render funds inaccessible.

To mitigate these risks, **developers must implement robust key management mechanisms** and **educate users on security best practices.**

Best Practices for Private Key Management

1. Use Hardware Wallets for Secure Key Storage

HARDWARE WALLETS, SUCH as **Ledger** and **Trezor,** store private keys in an isolated, offline environment, making them resistant to malware attacks.

Benefits of Hardware Wallets:

- **Offline storage** prevents online hacks.
- **Physical confirmation** is required for transactions.
- **PIN protection** adds an extra security layer.

Developers should encourage users to store high-value assets in hardware wallets instead of software-based wallets.

2. Avoid Storing Private Keys in Code or Configuration Files

DEVELOPERS MUST **never** hardcode private keys in repositories or application files. Even in private repositories, keys can be accidentally exposed.

Example of a Poor Practice:

CONST PRIVATE_KEY = "0x123456789abcdef..."; // ⍰ Bad practice

Instead, use **environment variables** or secure key vaults:

Secure Practice Using Environment Variables:

```
REQUIRE('DOTENV').CONFIG();

const privateKey = process.env.PRIVATE_KEY;
```

Secure Practice Using AWS Secrets Manager:

```
CONST AWS = REQUIRE('aws-sdk');

const secretsManager = new AWS.SecretsManager();

async function getPrivateKey() {

const data = await secretsManager.getSecretValue({ SecretId: 'MyPrivateKey' }).promise();

return data.SecretString;

}
```

By leveraging secret managers, developers prevent accidental exposure of sensitive data.

3. Implement Multi-Signature Wallets

MULTI-SIGNATURE (MULTI-sig) wallets require multiple private key signatures before executing a transaction. This enhances security for **high-value transactions and administrative accounts**.

Example: Deploying a Gnosis Safe Multi-Sig Wallet

```
// GNOSIS SAFE MULTI-Sig requires multiple owners to sign a transaction

contract MultiSigWallet {

address[] public owners;

uint public requiredSignatures;

constructor(address[] memory _owners, uint _requiredSignatures) {

require(_owners.length >= _requiredSignatures, "Not enough owners");

owners = _owners;

requiredSignatures = _requiredSignatures;

}

function executeTransaction() public {

// Logic to ensure multiple approvals before executing

}

}
```

Multi-sig wallets add an extra layer of security by **preventing a single point of failure**.

4. Use Hierarchical Deterministic (HD) Wallets

HD WALLETS GENERATE multiple addresses from a **single seed phrase**, reducing reliance on a single key. This is beneficial for applications that need to create **multiple addresses for users.**

Example: Generating Addresses with an HD Wallet

```
const bip39 = require("bip39");

const hdkey = require("ethereumjs-wallet/hdkey");

const mnemonic = bip39.generateMnemonic();

const seed = bip39.mnemonicToSeedSync(mnemonic);

const hdwallet = hdkey.fromMasterSeed(seed);

const key1 = hdwallet.derivePath("m/44'/60'/0'/0/0").getWallet();

const key2 = hdwallet.derivePath("m/44'/60'/0'/0/1").getWallet();

console.log("Address 1:", key1.getAddressString());

console.log("Address 2:", key2.getAddressString());
```

HD wallets allow applications to create multiple addresses while managing **a single backup seed.**

5. Encourage Users to Use Secure Passwords and 2FA

FOR DAPPS THAT REQUIRE authentication beyond blockchain transactions, **two-factor authentication (2FA)** should be enforced. Users should also be encouraged to:

- Use **strong, unique passwords.**

- Enable **biometric authentication** if available.
- Use a **password manager** for storing credentials securely.

6. Implement Secure Key Recovery Mechanisms

SINCE **lost private keys cannot be recovered**, DApps should provide **non-custodial key recovery options.**

Possible Recovery Strategies:

- **Social Recovery:** Trusted contacts approve recovery requests.
- **Shamir's Secret Sharing:** The private key is split into multiple parts, requiring a threshold to reconstruct.
- **Smart Contract-Based Recovery:** Users can define recovery conditions on-chain.

Example: Social Recovery Contract

```
CONTRACT SOCIALRECOVERY {
mapping(address => address[]) public guardians;
mapping(address => bool) public recoveryApproved;
function addGuardian(address _guardian) public {
guardians[msg.sender].push(_guardian);
}
```

```
function approveRecovery(address _user) public {

require(isGuardian(msg.sender, _user), "Not a guardian");

recoveryApproved[_user] = true;

}

function recoverAccount(address _user, address _newKey) public {

require(recoveryApproved[_user], "Recovery not approved");

// Assign new key to user

}

function isGuardian(address _guardian, address _user) public view returns (bool) {

for (uint i = 0; i < guardians[_user].length; i++) {

if (guardians[_user][i] == _guardian) return true;

}

return false;

}

}
```

This contract enables **trusted contacts to approve key recovery requests**, providing a **decentralized recovery mechanism**.

User Security in DApps

BEYOND PRIVATE KEY management, **DApps must implement security features** to protect users from phishing, scams, and unauthorized transactions.

1. Use Transaction Signing Warnings

DAPPS SHOULD DISPLAY **clear warnings** before users sign transactions.

Example: MetaMask Transaction Warning

```
CONST PROVIDER = NEW ethers.providers.Web3Provider(window.ethereum);

const signer = provider.getSigner();

const tx = {

to: "0xRecipientAddress",

value: ethers.utils.parseEther("1.0"),

data: "0x",

};

const message = `You are sending 1 ETH to 0xRecipientAddress. Do you confirm?`;

if (confirm(message)) {

await signer.sendTransaction(tx);

}
```

This ensures that users understand the consequences before signing.

2. Integrate Phishing Protection

DAPPS SHOULD MAINTAIN a **blacklist of malicious domains** and warn users before interacting with suspected phishing sites.

3. Enable Session Timeouts

AUTOMATICALLY LOGGING out users after inactivity reduces the risk of **session hijacking**.

Conclusion

PRIVATE KEY MANAGEMENT and user security are **foundational to blockchain security**. By implementing best practices such as **hardware wallets, multi-signature accounts, secure key storage, and non-custodial recovery options**, developers can **minimize risks and enhance user protection.**

DApps should integrate **secure authentication, transaction warnings, and phishing protection mechanisms** to safeguard users from threats. The responsibility for blockchain security **lies not only with developers but also with users**, and education on secure key management is essential for widespread blockchain adoption.

Regulatory and Compliance Considerations

THE DECENTRALIZED NATURE of blockchain technology and DApps presents significant regulatory challenges. Unlike traditional applications that operate within well-defined legal frameworks, blockchain applications often exist in a **gray area of regulation**, varying from country to country. Compliance with financial laws, data protection regulations, and anti-money laundering (AML) directives is crucial for ensuring that DApps remain legally compliant while maintaining decentralization.

This section explores the key regulatory considerations that developers must address when building DApps, including **AML and Know Your Customer (KYC) regulations, data privacy laws, securities regulations, and smart contract legal enforceability**.

Understanding the Importance of Regulatory Compliance

REGULATORY COMPLIANCE is essential for the following reasons:

1. **Avoiding Legal Penalties** – Governments can impose fines, restrict access, or ban non-compliant DApps.
2. **Ensuring User Protection** – Regulatory compliance ensures that users are protected from fraud, financial exploitation, and privacy breaches.
3. **Increasing Institutional Adoption** – Enterprises and financial institutions require regulatory clarity before adopting blockchain-based solutions.
4. **Preventing Exploitation by Criminals** – Proper compliance mechanisms help mitigate the risk of money laundering, fraud, and illicit activities.

By proactively addressing regulatory concerns, DApps can **gain legitimacy, foster trust, and facilitate mass adoption**.

Anti-Money Laundering (AML) and Know Your Customer (KYC) Regulations

GOVERNMENTS WORLDWIDE enforce **AML and KYC regulations** to combat financial crimes such as money laundering and terrorist financing. While blockchain technology is inherently transparent, pseudonymous transactions present challenges for regulatory compliance.

1. Understanding AML and KYC Requirements

- **AML regulations** require financial institutions to monitor and report suspicious transactions.
- **KYC policies** ensure that businesses verify user identities before granting access to financial services.

MANY JURISDICTIONS classify **crypto exchanges, DeFi platforms, and NFT marketplaces** as financial institutions, requiring them to implement AML and KYC procedures.

2. Challenges of Implementing AML/KYC in DApps

- **Privacy vs. Compliance** – Traditional AML/KYC processes require users to share personal data, conflicting with blockchain's decentralization and privacy goals.
- **Lack of Regulatory Clarity** – Regulations vary globally, making compliance complex for globally accessible DApps.
- **On-Chain Anonymity** – Many blockchain networks do not have built-in identity verification mechanisms.

3. Best Practices for AML/KYC Compliance in DApps

- **Integrate Decentralized Identity Solutions** – Use self-sovereign identity (SSI) platforms like **Civic** or **Bloom** to enable KYC without centralizing user data.

- **Use On-Chain Analysis Tools** – Platforms like **Chainalysis** and **Elliptic** help detect suspicious transactions and enforce AML policies.

- **Implement Tiered Access** – Allow small transactions without KYC, but require verification for large transactions.

- **Smart Contract-Based Compliance** – Develop **on-chain KYC solutions** where verified addresses interact with restricted contracts.

Example: Implementing an On-Chain KYC Whitelist

```
PRAGMA SOLIDITY ^0.8.0;

contract KYCWhitelist {

mapping(address => bool) public whitelisted;

function addWhitelisted(address user) public {

require(msg.sender == owner, "Only owner can whitelist");

whitelisted[user] = true;

}

function isWhitelisted(address user) public view returns (bool) {
```

```
return whitelisted[user];

}

}
```

This simple smart contract allows **only KYC-approved addresses** to access certain functionalities.

Data Protection and Privacy Laws

DAPPS THAT HANDLE **user data** must comply with global data protection laws such as:

- **General Data Protection Regulation (GDPR) (EU)**
- **California Consumer Privacy Act (CCPA) (USA)**
- **Personal Data Protection Act (PDPA) (Singapore)**

1. Challenges of Blockchain and Data Privacy Laws

- **Immutability vs. Right to be Forgotten** – GDPR grants users the right to erase personal data, conflicting with blockchain's immutable nature.
- **Data Storage Locations** – Many privacy laws require that personal data remain within specific jurisdictions.
- **Decentralized Data Ownership** – Unlike centralized apps, no single entity "owns" data in many DApps.

2. Best Practices for GDPR and Data Privacy Compliance

- **Minimize Data Collection** – Avoid storing personal data on-chain whenever possible.
- **Use Hashing Instead of Plain Storage** – Store user data off-chain and only keep cryptographic hashes on-chain.
- **Enable Data Encryption** – Use **zero-knowledge proofs (ZKPs)** to verify information without exposing raw data.
- **Implement Smart Contracts with Data Removal Capabilities** – If legal obligations arise, allow encrypted user data to be removed from external storage.

Example: Storing Encrypted User Data with Hashing

```
PRAGMA SOLIDITY ^0.8.0;

contract UserRegistry {

mapping(address => bytes32) private userHashes;

function storeUserData(string memory data) public {

userHashes[msg.sender] = keccak256(abi.encodePacked(data));

}

function getUserHash(address user) public view returns (bytes32) {

return userHashes[user];

}
```

```
}
```

This approach allows for **data verification without exposing raw personal information.**

Securities Regulations and Token Compliance

MANY DAPPS INVOLVE **token issuance**, which can trigger **securities regulations** depending on the token's characteristics.

1. How Regulators Determine If a Token is a Security

REGULATORS LIKE THE **U.S. Securities and Exchange Commission (SEC)** use the **Howey Test** to classify tokens:

- **Investment of money** – Users purchase tokens expecting value.
- **Expectation of profit** – Users anticipate financial returns.
- **Common enterprise** – Token value depends on project success.
- **Efforts of others** – Profits rely on the work of developers or a central entity.

If a token meets these criteria, it is classified as a **security**, requiring compliance with securities laws.

2. Best Practices for Token Compliance

- **Perform a Legal Review** – Work with legal experts to determine token classification.

- **Use Security Token Offerings (STOs)** – If classified as a security, register the token offering legally.

- **Restrict Access to Accredited Investors** – Use KYC and whitelisting mechanisms for legally compliant sales.

- **Comply with Tax Reporting Requirements** – Many jurisdictions require reporting of **capital gains and token-based earnings.**

Legal Enforceability of Smart Contracts

SMART CONTRACTS EXECUTE automatically on the blockchain, but **legal systems may not always recognize them as enforceable agreements.**

1. Challenges of Smart Contract Legality

- **Jurisdiction Issues** – Blockchain is global, but laws vary by country.

- **Code vs. Legal Contracts** – Some agreements require human interpretation, which smart contracts lack.

- **No Legal Recourse** – If an error occurs in an immutable smart contract, there may be no legal remedy.

2. Best Practices for Legal Recognition of Smart Contracts

- **Hybrid Smart Contracts** – Combine smart contract execution with legal agreements stored off-chain.

- **Use Legal-Tech Solutions** – Platforms like **OpenLaw** and **Mattereum** bridge blockchain and legal compliance.

- **Adopt DAO Governance for Dispute Resolution** – Use **Decentralized Arbitration** for contractual disagreements.

Example: Legal Agreement Embedded in a Smart Contract

```
CONTRACT LEGALCONTRACT {

string public agreementText;

address public partyA;

address public partyB;

constructor(string memory _agreement, address _partyA, address _partyB) {

agreementText = _agreement;

partyA = _partyA;

partyB = _partyB;

}

function signContract() public {

require(msg.sender == partyA || msg.sender == partyB, "Not authorized");

// Record signature on-chain

}

}
```

This contract links **legal agreements with on-chain verification.**

Conclusion

REGULATORY AND COMPLIANCE considerations are critical for **ensuring legal security and protecting users** in DApps. By proactively addressing **AML/KYC regulations, data privacy laws, securities compliance, and smart contract enforceability**, developers can build **sustainable, legally compliant blockchain applications**.

The decentralized nature of blockchain presents **regulatory challenges**, but by adopting **best practices such as KYC whitelisting, encryption, hybrid legal contracts, and DAO governance**, DApps can navigate the complex landscape of **global compliance while preserving decentralization**.

Chapter 9: Real-World DApp Development Case Studies

Decentralized Finance (DeFi) Applications

DECENTRALIZED FINANCE (DeFi) is one of the most impactful applications of blockchain technology, revolutionizing traditional financial systems by removing intermediaries and enabling permissionless, transparent, and secure transactions. DeFi applications provide financial services such as lending, borrowing, trading, staking, and yield farming without relying on banks or centralized institutions. This section explores the core components of DeFi, its benefits, challenges, and a step-by-step guide to building a simple DeFi application.

Understanding DeFi and Its Core Components

DEFI OPERATES ON BLOCKCHAIN networks such as Ethereum, Binance Smart Chain (BSC), and Solana, leveraging smart contracts to facilitate automated transactions without intermediaries. Some key components of the DeFi ecosystem include:

- **Decentralized Exchanges (DEXs):** Platforms like Uniswap, SushiSwap, and PancakeSwap allow users to trade cryptocurrencies without a centralized authority.

- **Lending and Borrowing Protocols:** Protocols such as Aave, Compound, and MakerDAO enable users to lend and borrow assets through smart contracts.

• **Stablecoins:** Cryptocurrencies like USDT, USDC, and DAI maintain a stable value by being pegged to fiat currencies or backed by collateral.

• **Yield Farming and Staking:** Users can earn rewards by providing liquidity or staking assets in DeFi protocols.

• **Synthetic Assets:** Platforms like Synthetix enable the creation of tokenized representations of real-world assets such as stocks and commodities.

Advantages of DeFi

DEFI OFFERS NUMEROUS advantages over traditional finance:

1. **Permissionless and Inclusive:** Anyone with an internet connection and a crypto wallet can access DeFi services without requiring approval from financial institutions.
2. **Transparency and Security:** Blockchain ensures that all transactions are immutable, transparent, and auditable.
3. **Lower Costs and Faster Transactions:** DeFi eliminates intermediaries, reducing transaction costs and settlement times.
4. **Programmability:** Smart contracts enable automated financial operations such as collateralized loans and interest payments.
5. **Censorship Resistance:** DeFi applications operate on decentralized networks, making them resistant to censorship and government control.

Challenges and Risks in DeFi

DESPITE ITS BENEFITS, DeFi comes with several risks and challenges:

- **Smart Contract Vulnerabilities:** Bugs or exploits in smart contracts can lead to significant losses.

- **Liquidity Risks:** Some DeFi platforms suffer from low liquidity, affecting trading efficiency.

- **Regulatory Uncertainty:** Governments are still formulating regulations for DeFi, which could impact its adoption and compliance requirements.

- **Impermanent Loss:** Liquidity providers in AMMs (Automated Market Makers) may suffer losses due to price fluctuations.

- **Scalability Issues:** Network congestion and high gas fees can make DeFi applications expensive and slow.

Building a Simple DeFi Lending Application

TO UNDERSTAND DEFI development practically, let's walk through the creation of a basic lending and borrowing smart contract using Solidity. This contract will allow users to deposit and borrow ERC-20 tokens.

1. Setting Up the Development Environment

ENSURE THAT YOU HAVE the necessary tools installed:

- **Node.js and npm** for package management.

- **Truffle or Hardhat** for smart contract development.

- **MetaMask** for wallet interactions.

- **Ganache** for local blockchain testing.

Install Hardhat:

npm install—save-dev hardhat

Initialize a Hardhat project:

npx hardhat

2. Writing the Lending Smart Contract

CREATE A NEW SOLIDITY file Lending.sol inside the contracts directory.

```
pragma solidity ^0.8.0;

import "@openzeppelin/contracts/token/ERC20/IERC20.sol";

contract LendingPlatform {

address public owner;

IERC20 public token;

mapping(address => uint256) public deposits;

mapping(address => uint256) public borrowings;

constructor(address _token) {

owner = msg.sender;

token = IERC20(_token);

}

function deposit(uint256 _amount) public {

require(_amount > 0, "Amount must be greater than zero");
```

```
token.transferFrom(msg.sender, address(this), _amount);
deposits[msg.sender] += _amount;
}
function borrow(uint256 _amount) public {
require(deposits[msg.sender] >= _amount, "Insufficient collateral");
borrowings[msg.sender] += _amount;
token.transfer(msg.sender, _amount);
}
function repay(uint256 _amount) public {
require(borrowings[msg.sender] >= _amount, "Invalid amount");
token.transferFrom(msg.sender, address(this), _amount);
borrowings[msg.sender] -= _amount;
}
function withdraw(uint256 _amount) public {
require(deposits[msg.sender] >= _amount, "Not enough funds");
require(borrowings[msg.sender] == 0, "Loan not fully repaid");
deposits[msg.sender] -= _amount;
token.transfer(msg.sender, _amount);
}
}
```

3. Deploying the Smart Contract

CREATE A DEPLOYMENT script deploy.js:

```
const { ethers } = require("hardhat");

async function main() {

const tokenAddress = "0xYourERC20TokenAddress";

const LendingPlatform = await ethers.getContractFactory("LendingPlatform");

const lendingPlatform = await LendingPlatform.deploy(tokenAddress);

console.log("Lending Platform deployed at:", lendingPlatform.address);

}

main()

.then(() => process.exit(0))

.catch((error) => {

console.error(error);

process.exit(1);

});
```

Run the deployment script:

```
npx hardhat run scripts/deploy.js—network rinkeby
```

4. Integrating with a Frontend

TO INTERACT WITH THE lending platform from a frontend, use **Web3.js** or **Ethers.js**.

Example using **Ethers.js**:

```
import { ethers } from "ethers";

const contractAddress = "0xYourLendingPlatformAddress";

const abi = [...]; // ABI from compiled contract

const provider = new ethers.providers.Web3Provider(window.ethereum);

const signer = provider.getSigner();

const contract = new ethers.Contract(contractAddress, abi, signer);

async function deposit(amount) {

const tx = await contract.deposit(ethers.utils.parseUnits(amount, 18));

await tx.wait();

console.log("Deposit successful!");

}
```

5. Testing the Smart Contract

TO ENSURE SECURITY, write unit tests using **Chai and Mocha** in test/Lending.test.js:

```
const { expect } = require("chai");
```

```
describe("Lending Platform", function () {

let token, lendingPlatform, owner, user;

beforeEach(async function () {

const Token = await ethers.getContractFactory("MockERC20");

token = await Token.deploy();

await token.deployed();

const LendingPlatform = await
ethers.getContractFactory("LendingPlatform");

lendingPlatform = await LendingPlatform.deploy(token.address);

await lendingPlatform.deployed();

});

it("Should allow users to deposit tokens", async function () {

await token.approve(lendingPlatform.address, 1000);

await lendingPlatform.deposit(1000);

expect(await
lendingPlatform.deposits(owner.address)).to.equal(1000);

});

});
```

Run the tests:

```
npx hardhat test
```

Conclusion

THIS SECTION PROVIDED an in-depth look at DeFi applications, highlighting their significance, benefits, and challenges. We also built a simple DeFi lending platform using Solidity and deployed it using Hardhat. This project demonstrates how smart contracts can be leveraged to create permissionless financial systems, enabling users to interact with blockchain-based lending and borrowing mechanisms securely.

As DeFi continues to evolve, developers must stay updated with best practices, security protocols, and emerging innovations such as Layer 2 scaling solutions, cross-chain interoperability, and regulatory frameworks to build robust and compliant applications.

Non-Fungible Token (NFT) Marketplaces

NON-FUNGIBLE TOKENS (NFTs) have transformed the digital asset landscape by enabling the ownership and trade of unique, verifiable assets on the blockchain. Unlike cryptocurrencies, which are fungible and interchangeable, NFTs represent ownership of digital or physical assets, including art, music, virtual real estate, and in-game items. This section explores the fundamentals of NFTs, their technical underpinnings, key components of NFT marketplaces, challenges, and a step-by-step guide to building a simple NFT marketplace.

Understanding NFTs and Their Importance

NFTS ARE DIGITAL ASSETS that are stored on blockchain networks such as Ethereum, Solana, Binance Smart Chain (BSC), and Flow. They use **smart contracts** to ensure ownership, provenance, and scarcity. Key features of NFTs include:

- **Uniqueness:** Each NFT is distinct and cannot be replicated.
- **Verifiable Ownership:** Ownership is stored on a blockchain and can be publicly verified.
- **Indivisibility:** NFTs cannot be divided into smaller units like cryptocurrencies.
- **Interoperability:** NFTs can be transferred across different platforms and applications.

NFTs are primarily used in digital art, gaming, virtual real estate, and music licensing. The popularity of projects such as Bored Ape Yacht Club (BAYC), CryptoPunks, and Axie Infinity demonstrates the vast potential of NFTs.

Core Components of an NFT Marketplace

AN NFT MARKETPLACE is a decentralized platform that enables users to mint, buy, sell, and trade NFTs. The essential components of an NFT marketplace include:

1. **Smart Contracts:** Handle the minting, ownership transfers, and royalty enforcement.
2. **Token Standards:** Utilize standards such as **ERC-721** and **ERC-1155** for Ethereum-based NFTs.
3. **Decentralized Storage:** Store metadata and assets using **IPFS (InterPlanetary File System)** or **Arweave**.
4. **Wallet Integration:** Support for wallets like **MetaMask, WalletConnect, and Coinbase Wallet**.
5. **Frontend Interface:** A user-friendly UI for browsing, purchasing, and listing NFTs.

Challenges in NFT Marketplaces

DESPITE THEIR GROWTH, NFT marketplaces face several challenges:

- **Scalability Issues:** High gas fees and network congestion on Ethereum.
- **Security Concerns:** Smart contract vulnerabilities, phishing attacks, and fraud.
- **Legal and Copyright Issues:** Unauthorized minting of copyrighted content.
- **Environmental Impact:** Proof-of-Work (PoW) networks consume high energy.

Building a Simple NFT Marketplace

IN THIS SECTION, WE will build a basic NFT marketplace using **Solidity, Hardhat, Ethers.js, and React**.

1. Setting Up the Development Environment

FIRST, INSTALL THE necessary dependencies:

npm install—save-dev hardhat ethers @openzeppelin/contracts dotenv

Initialize a Hardhat project:

npx hardhat

2. Writing the NFT Smart Contract

CREATE A SOLIDITY FILE NFTMarketplace.sol inside the contracts directory.

```
pragma solidity ^0.8.0;

import "@openzeppelin/contracts/token/ERC721/extensions/ERC721URIStorage.sol";

import "@openzeppelin/contracts/access/Ownable.sol";

import "@openzeppelin/contracts/utils/Counters.sol";

contract NFTMarketplace is ERC721URIStorage, Ownable {

using Counters for Counters.Counter;

Counters.Counter private _tokenIds;

mapping(uint256 => uint256) public prices;

mapping(uint256 => bool) public listedTokens;

event Minted(uint256 tokenId, string tokenURI, address owner);

event Listed(uint256 tokenId, uint256 price);

event Sold(uint256 tokenId, address buyer, uint256 price);

constructor() ERC721("NFT Marketplace", "NFTM") {}

function mintNFT(string memory tokenURI) public returns (uint256) {

_tokenIds.increment();

uint256 newItemId = _tokenIds.current();
```

```
_mint(msg.sender, newItemId);
_setTokenURI(newItemId, tokenURI);
emit Minted(newItemId, tokenURI, msg.sender);
return newItemId;
}
function listNFT(uint256 tokenId, uint256 price) public {
require(ownerOf(tokenId) == msg.sender, "Not the owner");
require(price > 0, "Price must be greater than zero");
prices[tokenId] = price;
listedTokens[tokenId] = true;
emit Listed(tokenId, price);
}
function buyNFT(uint256 tokenId) public payable {
require(listedTokens[tokenId], "NFT not listed for sale");
require(msg.value == prices[tokenId], "Incorrect value sent");
address seller = ownerOf(tokenId);
_transfer(seller, msg.sender, tokenId);
payable(seller).transfer(msg.value);
listedTokens[tokenId] = false;
emit Sold(tokenId, msg.sender, prices[tokenId]);
```

```
}
}
```

3. Deploying the Smart Contract

CREATE A DEPLOY.JS script inside the scripts directory:

```
const { ethers } = require("hardhat");
async function main() {
const NFTMarketplace = await ethers.getContractFactory("NFTMarketplace");
const nftMarketplace = await NFTMarketplace.deploy();
console.log("NFT Marketplace deployed at:", nftMarketplace.address);
}
main()
.then(() => process.exit(0))
.catch((error) => {
console.error(error);
process.exit(1);
});
```

Deploy the contract:

```
npx hardhat run scripts/deploy.js—network rinkeby
```

4. Integrating the Frontend

USING REACT AND ETHERS.js, connect to the smart contract.

Example using **Ethers.js**:

```
import { ethers } from "ethers";

import NFTMarketplaceABI from "./NFTMarketplaceABI.json";

const contractAddress = "0xYourContractAddress";

const provider = new ethers.providers.Web3Provider(window.ethereum);

const signer = provider.getSigner();

const contract = new ethers.Contract(contractAddress, NFTMarketplaceABI, signer);

async function mintNFT(tokenURI) {

const tx = await contract.mintNFT(tokenURI);

await tx.wait();

console.log("NFT minted successfully!");

}

async function listNFT(tokenId, price) {

const tx = await contract.listNFT(tokenId, ethers.utils.parseEther(price));

await tx.wait();

console.log("NFT listed for sale!");
```

}

5. Interacting with the Smart Contract

TO MINT, LIST, AND buy NFTs:

await mintNFT("https://your-metadata-url.com");

await listNFT(1, "0.05");

await buyNFT(1, { value: ethers.utils.parseEther("0.05") });

6. Testing the NFT Marketplace

CREATE UNIT TESTS IN test/NFTMarketplace.test.js:

const { expect } = require("chai");

describe("NFT Marketplace", function () {

let NFTMarketplace, nftMarketplace, owner, user;

beforeEach(async function () {

NFTMarketplace = await ethers.getContractFactory("NFTMarketplace");

nftMarketplace = await NFTMarketplace.deploy();

await nftMarketplace.deployed();

});

it("Should mint an NFT", async function () {

await nftMarketplace.mintNFT("https://example.com/nft");

```
expect(await
nftMarketplace.tokenURI(1)).to.equal("https://example.com/nft");

});

it("Should list an NFT", async function () {

await nftMarketplace.mintNFT("https://example.com/nft");

await nftMarketplace.listNFT(1, ethers.utils.parseEther("0.1"));

expect(await
nftMarketplace.prices(1)).to.equal(ethers.utils.parseEther("0.1"));

});

it("Should allow purchase of an NFT", async function () {

await nftMarketplace.mintNFT("https://example.com/nft");

await nftMarketplace.listNFT(1, ethers.utils.parseEther("0.1"));

await nftMarketplace.buyNFT(1, { value:
ethers.utils.parseEther("0.1") });

expect(await nftMarketplace.ownerOf(1)).to.equal(user.address);

});

});
```

Run the tests:

```
npx hardhat test
```

Conclusion

THIS SECTION PROVIDED an in-depth look at NFT marketplaces, exploring their technical foundations and challenges.

We built a basic NFT marketplace using Solidity and deployed it using Hardhat. This project demonstrates how developers can create decentralized platforms for minting, buying, and selling NFTs, driving innovation in digital ownership and blockchain technology. As the NFT ecosystem evolves, future improvements will focus on scalability, interoperability, and user-friendly experiences to enhance mainstream adoption.

Decentralized Social Networks and Communication Platforms

DECENTRALIZED SOCIAL networks and communication platforms aim to provide users with censorship-resistant, secure, and user-controlled online interactions. Traditional social media platforms such as Facebook, Twitter, and Instagram operate under centralized authorities that control data, monetization, and content visibility. In contrast, decentralized social networks leverage blockchain technology to ensure transparency, data ownership, and resistance to censorship.

Key Features of Decentralized Social Networks

DECENTRALIZED SOCIAL networks focus on user empowerment and privacy. The core features include:

- **Censorship Resistance:** No central authority can delete or manipulate user content arbitrarily.

- **Data Ownership:** Users control their content, identity, and personal data without intermediaries.

- **Tokenization and Monetization:** Platforms enable rewards through cryptocurrencies or token-based economies.

- **Decentralized Identity (DID):** Users authenticate using blockchain-based identities instead of relying on centralized databases.

- **End-to-End Encryption:** Ensures privacy in messaging and data sharing.

Examples of decentralized social networks include **Mastodon, Peepeth, Lens Protocol, and Minds**, each built using different blockchain architectures and decentralized storage solutions.

Challenges in Decentralized Social Networks

DESPITE THE BENEFITS, these platforms face several challenges:

- **Scalability Issues:** High transaction costs and network congestion on blockchains can hinder user experience.

- **Moderation and Content Control:** Lack of centralized moderation can lead to spam, misinformation, and abusive content.

- **User Experience (UX):** Decentralized applications (DApps) often lack the smoothness and ease of use of traditional platforms.

- **Regulatory Uncertainty:** Governments may impose regulations on decentralized content-sharing platforms.

Building a Simple Decentralized Social Network

IN THIS SECTION, WE will build a simple decentralized social media platform that allows users to **post messages, interact with posts, and own their data**. We will use **Solidity for smart**

contracts, IPFS for decentralized storage, and React with Web3.js for the frontend.

1. Setting Up the Development Environment

INSTALL NECESSARY DEPENDENCIES:

npm install—save-dev hardhat ethers @openzeppelin/contracts dotenv

Initialize a Hardhat project:

npx hardhat

2. Writing the Smart Contract

CREATE A NEW SOLIDITY file SocialNetwork.sol inside the contracts directory.

pragma solidity ^0.8.0;

import "@openzeppelin/contracts/access/Ownable.sol";

contract SocialNetwork is Ownable {

struct Post {

uint256 id;

string content;

address author;

uint256 timestamp;

}

```
Post[] public posts;

mapping(uint256 => address) public postOwners;

event PostCreated(uint256 id, string content, address author, uint256 timestamp);

function createPost(string memory _content) public {

uint256 postId = posts.length;

posts.push(Post(postId, _content, msg.sender, block.timestamp));

postOwners[postId] = msg.sender;

emit PostCreated(postId, _content, msg.sender, block.timestamp);

}

function getAllPosts() public view returns (Post[] memory) {

return posts;

}

}
```

3. Deploying the Smart Contract

CREATE A DEPLOY.JS script inside the scripts directory:

```
const { ethers } = require("hardhat");

async function main() {

const SocialNetwork = await ethers.getContractFactory("SocialNetwork");
```

```
const socialNetwork = await SocialNetwork.deploy();
console.log("Social Network deployed at:", socialNetwork.address);
}
main()
.then(() => process.exit(0))
.catch((error) => {
console.error(error);
process.exit(1);
});
```

Deploy the contract:

```
npx hardhat run scripts/deploy.js—network rinkeby
```

4. Integrating the Frontend

USING REACT AND ETHERS.js, connect to the smart contract.

```
import { ethers } from "ethers";
import SocialNetworkABI from "./SocialNetworkABI.json";
const contractAddress = "0xYourContractAddress";
const provider = new ethers.providers.Web3Provider(window.ethereum);
const signer = provider.getSigner();
```

```
const contract = new ethers.Contract(contractAddress, SocialNetworkABI, signer);

async function createPost(content) {

const tx = await contract.createPost(content);

await tx.wait();

console.log("Post created successfully!");

}

async function getAllPosts() {

const posts = await contract.getAllPosts();

console.log("All Posts:", posts);

}
```

5. Storing Content on IPFS

SINCE BLOCKCHAIN TRANSACTIONS are costly for storing large data, we will use IPFS to store post content.

Install ipfs-http-client:

```
npm install ipfs-http-client
```

Upload content to IPFS:

```
import { create } from "ipfs-http-client";

const ipfs = create({ url: "https://ipfs.infura.io:5001/api/v0" });

async function uploadToIPFS(content) {
```

```
const result = await ipfs.add(content);

return `https://ipfs.infura.io/ipfs/${result.path}`;

}

async function createPost(content) {

const ipfsUrl = await uploadToIPFS(content);

const tx = await contract.createPost(ipfsUrl);

await tx.wait();

console.log("Post created successfully!");

}
```

6. Implementing User Authentication

TO PROVIDE USERS WITH decentralized authentication, we use **Ethereum wallets like MetaMask**.

```
async function connectWallet() {

if (window.ethereum) {

const accounts = await window.ethereum.request({ method: "eth_requestAccounts" });

console.log("Connected Wallet:", accounts[0]);

} else {

console.log("Please install MetaMask.");

}
```

}

7. Testing the Smart Contract

CREATE UNIT TESTS IN test/SocialNetwork.test.js:

```
const { expect } = require("chai");

describe("Social Network", function () {

let SocialNetwork, socialNetwork, owner, user;

beforeEach(async function () {

SocialNetwork = await ethers.getContractFactory("SocialNetwork");

socialNetwork = await SocialNetwork.deploy();

await socialNetwork.deployed();

});

it("Should allow users to create a post", async function () {

await socialNetwork.createPost("Hello, world!");

const posts = await socialNetwork.getAllPosts();

expect(posts.length).to.equal(1);

expect(posts[0].content).to.equal("Hello, world!");

});

});
```

Run the tests:

npx hardhat test

Future Enhancements

TO IMPROVE THE DECENTRALIZED social network, we can add:

- **User Profiles:** Implement DID-based identity management.
- **Comment and Like Features:** Enable social interactions through smart contracts.
- **Tokenized Rewards:** Introduce ERC-20 tokens to reward active users.
- **Decentralized Content Moderation:** Use DAO-based governance for content regulation.

Conclusion

THIS SECTION EXPLORED decentralized social networks, their challenges, and benefits. We built a simple decentralized social media platform using Solidity, IPFS, and React, enabling users to post content and interact with blockchain-based data. Future improvements could integrate more scalable Layer 2 solutions, better user experience features, and decentralized governance mechanisms to enhance adoption.

Supply Chain and Enterprise Blockchain Solutions

BLOCKCHAIN TECHNOLOGY has significantly disrupted traditional supply chain management by enhancing transparency, security, and efficiency. Supply chain solutions built on blockchain enable companies to track goods, authenticate products, and ensure trust among stakeholders. Unlike traditional systems, which rely on centralized databases and intermediaries, blockchain-based supply chains create immutable, verifiable records accessible by all participants.

Key Benefits of Blockchain in Supply Chains

ENTERPRISE BLOCKCHAIN solutions provide several advantages for supply chain management:

- **Transparency and Traceability:** Every transaction is recorded on an immutable ledger, allowing stakeholders to track product movements in real-time.

- **Security and Fraud Prevention:** Cryptographic security reduces counterfeiting and fraudulent transactions.

- **Efficiency and Cost Reduction:** Automation through smart contracts eliminates paperwork and intermediaries, reducing operational costs.

- **Decentralization:** Unlike centralized supply chain management systems, blockchain-based solutions allow for trustless collaboration.

- **Compliance and Auditing:** Regulatory requirements can be embedded into smart contracts, ensuring automated compliance.

Challenges in Blockchain Supply Chain Implementation

DESPITE ITS BENEFITS, blockchain adoption in supply chain management comes with certain challenges:

- **Integration with Legacy Systems:** Many companies still use traditional supply chain software that does not support blockchain integration.
- **Scalability Issues:** Public blockchains can suffer from congestion and high transaction fees.
- **Data Privacy Concerns:** Sensitive company data may require additional encryption and access control.
- **Interoperability:** Different blockchain platforms may struggle to communicate with one another.
- **Adoption Barriers:** Resistance from stakeholders and high initial costs can slow adoption.

Building a Blockchain-Based Supply Chain Solution

IN THIS SECTION, WE will develop a **basic supply chain smart contract** that enables manufacturers, distributors, and retailers to track product shipments. This solution will use **Solidity, IPFS for product metadata storage, and React with Ethers.js for the frontend**.

1. Setting Up the Development Environment

INSTALL THE NECESSARY dependencies:

npm install—save-dev hardhat ethers @openzeppelin/contracts dotenv

Initialize a Hardhat project:

npx hardhat

2. Writing the Smart Contract

CREATE A SOLIDITY FILE SupplyChain.sol inside the contracts directory.

pragma solidity ^0.8.0;

import "@openzeppelin/contracts/access/Ownable.sol";

contract SupplyChain is Ownable {

enum Status { Created, InTransit, Delivered }

struct Product {

uint256 id;

string name;

string metadataHash;

address manufacturer;

address distributor;

address retailer;

Status status;

}

```
mapping(uint256 => Product) public products;

uint256 public productCounter;

event ProductCreated(uint256 id, string name, address manufacturer);

event ProductShipped(uint256 id, address distributor);

event ProductDelivered(uint256 id, address retailer);

function createProduct(string memory _name, string memory _metadataHash) public {

productCounter++;

products[productCounter] = Product(productCounter, _name, _metadataHash, msg.sender, address(0), address(0), Status.Created);

emit ProductCreated(productCounter, _name, msg.sender);

}

function shipProduct(uint256 _productId, address distributor) public {

require(products[_productId].manufacturer == msg.sender, "Only the manufacturer can ship this product.");

products[_productId].distributor = _distributor;

products[_productId].status = Status.InTransit;

emit ProductShipped(_productId, _distributor);

}
```

```
function deliverProduct(uint256 _productId, address _retailer) public {

require(products[_productId].distributor == msg.sender, "Only the distributor can deliver this product.");

products[_productId].retailer = _retailer;

products[_productId].status = Status.Delivered;

emit ProductDelivered(_productId, _retailer);

}

function getProduct(uint256 _productId) public view returns (Product memory) {

return products[_productId];

}

}
```

3. Deploying the Smart Contract

CREATE A DEPLOY.JS script inside the scripts directory:

```
const { ethers } = require("hardhat");

async function main() {

const SupplyChain = await ethers.getContractFactory("SupplyChain");

const supplyChain = await SupplyChain.deploy();

console.log("Supply Chain contract deployed at:", supplyChain.address);
```

```
}
main()
.then(() => process.exit(0))
.catch((error) => {
console.error(error);
process.exit(1);
});
```

Deploy the contract:

```
npx hardhat run scripts/deploy.js—network rinkeby
```

4. Integrating with IPFS for Metadata Storage

SINCE BLOCKCHAIN STORAGE is expensive, we will store product metadata (such as manufacturing details, expiration dates, and tracking data) on IPFS.

Install ipfs-http-client:

```
npm install ipfs-http-client
```

Upload metadata to IPFS:

```
import { create } from "ipfs-http-client";
const ipfs = create({ url: "https://ipfs.infura.io:5001/api/v0" });
async function uploadToIPFS(metadata) {
const result = await ipfs.add(JSON.stringify(metadata));
```

```
return `https://ipfs.infura.io/ipfs/${result.path}`;
}
```

5. Integrating with the Frontend

USING **React and Ethers.js,** we connect to the smart contract.

```
import { ethers } from "ethers";
import SupplyChainABI from "./SupplyChainABI.json";
const contractAddress = "0xYourContractAddress";
const provider = new ethers.providers.Web3Provider(window.ethereum);
const signer = provider.getSigner();
const contract = new ethers.Contract(contractAddress, SupplyChainABI, signer);
async function createProduct(name, metadata) {
const metadataUrl = await uploadToIPFS(metadata);
const tx = await contract.createProduct(name, metadataUrl);
await tx.wait();
console.log("Product created successfully!");
}
async function shipProduct(productId, distributorAddress) {
const tx = await contract.shipProduct(productId, distributorAddress);
```

```
await tx.wait();

console.log("Product shipped!");

}

async function deliverProduct(productId, retailerAddress) {

const tx = await contract.deliverProduct(productId, retailerAddress);

await tx.wait();

console.log("Product delivered!");

}
```

6. Testing the Smart Contract

CREATE UNIT TESTS IN test/SupplyChain.test.js:

```
const { expect } = require("chai");

describe("Supply Chain", function () {

let SupplyChain, supplyChain, owner, manufacturer, distributor, retailer;

beforeEach(async function () {

SupplyChain = await ethers.getContractFactory("SupplyChain");

supplyChain = await SupplyChain.deploy();

await supplyChain.deployed();

});
```

```
it("Should create a product", async function () {

await supplyChain.createProduct("Laptop", "Qm1234567890abcdef");

const product = await supplyChain.getProduct(1);

expect(product.name).to.equal("Laptop");

});

it("Should allow manufacturer to ship a product", async function () {

await supplyChain.createProduct("Laptop", "Qm1234567890abcdef");

await supplyChain.shipProduct(1, distributor.address);

const product = await supplyChain.getProduct(1);

expect(product.status).to.equal(1); // Status.InTransit

});

it("Should allow distributor to deliver a product", async function () {

await supplyChain.createProduct("Laptop", "Qm1234567890abcdef");

await supplyChain.shipProduct(1, distributor.address);

await supplyChain.deliverProduct(1, retailer.address);

const product = await supplyChain.getProduct(1);

expect(product.status).to.equal(2); // Status.Delivered

});
```

```
});
```

Run the tests:

```
npx hardhat test
```

Future Enhancements

TO IMPROVE THE SUPPLY chain solution, we can integrate:

- **QR Code Scanning:** To enable easy tracking and verification.
- **Tokenized Payments:** Automate payments using stablecoins or utility tokens.
- **Multi-Signature Approval:** Add governance for product authenticity validation.
- **Decentralized Autonomous Organization (DAO):** Implement community-driven supply chain decisions.

Conclusion

THIS SECTION EXPLORED how blockchain enhances supply chain management. We built a **basic supply chain smart contract** and demonstrated how to integrate IPFS for metadata storage. Blockchain-powered supply chains can **increase transparency, reduce fraud, and enhance efficiency**, making them ideal for **food tracking, pharmaceuticals, and luxury goods authentication**. Future improvements could include **IoT integration, Layer 2 scaling, and AI-powered analytics** to further optimize the system.

Chapter 10: Future Trends and Innovations in Blockchain Development

The Rise of Web3 and Decentralized Identity

Introduction

THE TRANSITION FROM Web2 to Web3 represents a paradigm shift in how the internet operates, focusing on decentralization, user sovereignty, and trustless interactions. Web3 is a decentralized web built on blockchain technology, where users have control over their data, identities, and digital assets. One of the most crucial aspects of this evolution is **decentralized identity (DID)**, which seeks to eliminate reliance on centralized authorities for identity verification and management.

Traditional identity systems depend on centralized entities such as governments, corporations, or social media platforms to issue and verify identities. This approach has several drawbacks, including privacy risks, data breaches, and censorship concerns. Decentralized identity, on the other hand, enables individuals to own and control their identities without intermediaries. This is achieved through blockchain-based identity solutions that leverage cryptographic proofs and decentralized identifiers.

This section delves into the fundamentals of decentralized identity, its components, protocols, and how it integrates into Web3. It also explores real-world use cases and implementation strategies.

Understanding Decentralized Identity

DECENTRALIZED IDENTITY (DID) is an identity framework where individuals or entities create, own, and manage their digital identities without a central authority. The core principles of decentralized identity include:

- **Self-Sovereignty**: Users control their identity without relying on third-party providers.
- **Interoperability**: DIDs can be used across different applications, blockchains, and platforms.
- **Privacy-Preserving**: Users can share only the necessary information without exposing personal data.
- **Security and Verifiability**: Identity information is cryptographically secured and verifiable on a public ledger.

A decentralized identity system typically consists of the following components:

1. **Decentralized Identifiers (DIDs)** – Unique identifiers that are registered on a blockchain.
2. **Verifiable Credentials (VCs)** – Digital certificates issued by trusted parties that can be cryptographically verified.
3. **Identity Wallets** – Software tools that allow users to manage their DIDs and credentials.
4. **Decentralized Identity Providers** – Services that facilitate the issuance and verification of decentralized identities.

How Decentralized Identifiers (DIDs) Work

DECENTRALIZED IDENTIFIERS (DIDs) are the foundation of decentralized identity. A DID is a globally unique identifier that is registered on a blockchain or distributed ledger. Unlike traditional identifiers (such as email addresses or usernames), a DID is controlled by the user and does not require a centralized registry.

A DID document contains metadata about the identity, including:

- A unique identifier (DID string)
- Public keys associated with the identity
- Authentication mechanisms
- Service endpoints

A sample DID document stored on a blockchain might look like this:

```
{
"id": "did:example:123456789abcdefghi",
"verificationMethod": [
{
"id": "did:example:123456789abcdefghi#keys-1",
"type": "Ed25519VerificationKey2018",
"controller": "did:example:123456789abcdefghi",
"publicKeyBase58":
"3J98t1WpEZ73CNmQviecrnyiWrnqRhWNLy"
```

```
}
],
"authentication": [
"did:example:123456789abcdefghi#keys-1"
],
"service": [
{
"id": "did:example:123456789abcdefghi#vc",
"type": "VerifiableCredentialService",
"serviceEndpoint": "https://example.com/credentials"
}
]
}
```

This document provides cryptographic proof that the identity is controlled by the associated private key.

Verifiable Credentials (VCs) and Selective Disclosure

VERIFIABLE CREDENTIALS (VCs) are digital statements that prove specific claims about an individual or entity. These credentials are signed by an issuer and can be verified by any party without the need to contact the issuer. Examples of verifiable credentials include:

- A university degree certificate

- A government-issued identity card
- A proof of age verification

A key feature of verifiable credentials is **selective disclosure**, which allows users to share only necessary information without exposing the entire credential. This is facilitated through **zero-knowledge proofs (ZKPs)**, which enable verification of a claim without revealing the underlying data.

For example, instead of sharing a full ID document to prove one's age, a user can share a cryptographic proof stating that they are over 18.

Identity Wallets and User Experience

TO INTERACT WITH A decentralized identity system, users require **identity wallets**. These wallets store DIDs, verifiable credentials, and cryptographic keys. Some notable identity wallets include:

- **MetaMask (with decentralized identity extensions)**
- **uPort**
- **Sovrin Wallet**
- **Microsoft Identity Overlay Network (ION)**

A good decentralized identity wallet must have:

- **Private key management** – Securely storing cryptographic keys.
- **Interoperability** – Support for multiple DID methods.

- **User-friendly interface** – Simplified onboarding and interaction.

Decentralized Identity Protocols and Standards

SEVERAL PROTOCOLS AND standards are being developed to support decentralized identity. Some of the most notable include:

1. **W3C Decentralized Identifiers (DIDs)** – A standard for decentralized identity on the web.
2. **W3C Verifiable Credentials (VCs)** – A framework for verifiable claims.
3. **DIDComm** – A communication protocol for secure messaging between decentralized identities.
4. **Sovrin and Hyperledger Indy** – Open-source blockchain solutions for identity.
5. **Microsoft ION (Identity Overlay Network)** – A decentralized identity solution built on Bitcoin.

These standards ensure that decentralized identities are portable, verifiable, and usable across various ecosystems.

Real-World Use Cases of Decentralized Identity

1. Digital Identity for Individuals

- Users can create and manage their identity without relying on centralized identity providers.

- Enables a universal login system across different platforms.

2. KYC and AML Compliance

- Financial institutions can verify identities without storing sensitive personal data.

- Reduces the risk of identity theft and fraud.

3. Decentralized Voting Systems

- Governments and organizations can implement tamper-proof voting mechanisms.

- Eliminates voter fraud and enhances transparency.

4. Healthcare and Medical Records

- Patients can control their medical history and grant access to healthcare providers when needed.

- Ensures data privacy and reduces administrative inefficiencies.

5. Cross-Border Identity Verification

- Enables seamless identity verification across different countries and institutions.

- Reduces the need for physical documents and manual verifications.

Challenges and Future of Decentralized Identity

DESPITE ITS POTENTIAL, decentralized identity faces several challenges:

- **Adoption Barriers** – Traditional institutions are slow to adopt blockchain-based identity solutions.

- **Regulatory Concerns** – Governments and policymakers are still developing regulations for decentralized identity.

- **User Experience** – Managing cryptographic keys can be complex for non-technical users.

However, the future of decentralized identity is promising. With advancements in blockchain scalability, zero-knowledge proofs, and improved user interfaces, decentralized identity will likely become the standard for digital identity management.

Conclusion

DECENTRALIZED IDENTITY is a foundational component of Web3, enabling users to have full control over their digital presence. By leveraging blockchain technology, DIDs and verifiable credentials offer a secure, private, and interoperable identity system. As adoption increases, decentralized identity will play a crucial role in digital identity management, financial services, healthcare, and many other industries. The shift towards self-sovereign identity marks a significant step towards a more open, secure, and user-centric internet.

Zero-Knowledge Proofs and Privacy Enhancements

Introduction

PRIVACY IS ONE OF THE most critical concerns in blockchain technology. While public blockchains offer transparency and immutability, they also expose transaction details to anyone with access to the network. This lack of privacy presents challenges for individuals, enterprises, and governments that require confidentiality in transactions and data exchanges. **Zero-knowledge proofs (ZKPs)** have emerged as a revolutionary cryptographic technique to address these privacy concerns while maintaining security and decentralization.

Zero-knowledge proofs enable one party (the prover) to prove to another party (the verifier) that a statement is true without revealing any specific details about the statement itself. This concept has far-reaching applications in **blockchain transactions, identity verification, confidential data sharing, and secure computations**.

This section explores the fundamentals of zero-knowledge proofs, different types of ZKPs, how they enhance privacy in blockchain applications, and real-world use cases. We will also discuss implementation strategies and the challenges associated with ZKP adoption.

Fundamentals of Zero-Knowledge Proofs

ZERO-KNOWLEDGE PROOFS allow one party to prove knowledge of a fact without disclosing any information beyond the validity of the statement. The concept was first introduced in the 1980s by Shafi Goldwasser, Silvio Micali, and Charles Rackoff.

For a proof to be considered **zero-knowledge**, it must satisfy three key properties:

1. **Completeness** – If the statement is true, an honest verifier will be convinced by an honest prover.
2. **Soundness** – If the statement is false, a dishonest prover cannot convince an honest verifier that it is true.

3. **Zero-Knowledge** – The verifier learns nothing beyond the fact that the statement is true.

A simple analogy for zero-knowledge proofs is the "Where's Waldo?" problem. Suppose you want to prove that you have found Waldo in a picture without revealing his exact location. You could cover the entire image except for Waldo, demonstrating that you know where he is without exposing any other details. This is the essence of ZKPs.

Types of Zero-Knowledge Proofs

THERE ARE TWO PRIMARY types of zero-knowledge proofs used in blockchain applications:

1. Interactive Zero-Knowledge Proofs

- Requires multiple rounds of interaction between the prover and verifier.
- Not ideal for large-scale decentralized applications.
- Example: The classic "Ali Baba Cave" example demonstrates interactive proofs where a prover convinces a verifier of knowledge by following specific instructions.

2. Non-Interactive Zero-Knowledge Proofs (NIZKs)

- Eliminates the need for repeated interaction.
- More suitable for blockchain and cryptographic applications.
- Example: **zk-SNARKs (Zero-Knowledge Succinct Non-Interactive Arguments of Knowledge)** and

zk-STARKs (Zero-Knowledge Scalable Transparent Arguments of Knowledge).

ZK-SNARKS ARE WIDELY used in privacy-focused cryptocurrencies like Zcash, while zk-STARKs provide enhanced scalability and security benefits.

Zero-Knowledge Proofs in Blockchain Privacy

ZERO-KNOWLEDGE PROOFS significantly enhance privacy and confidentiality in blockchain networks. Some key applications include:

1. Private Transactions

- Traditional blockchain transactions expose sender/receiver details and transaction amounts.
- ZKPs enable transactions to be verified without revealing transaction details.
- Example: **Zcash** uses zk-SNARKs to facilitate shielded transactions, allowing users to prove transaction validity without exposing amounts or addresses.

2. Anonymous Identity Verification

- Users can prove their identity attributes (e.g., age, citizenship) without exposing unnecessary personal data.
- Example: A user can prove they are above 18 without revealing their date of birth.

3. Secure Voting Systems

- Ensures a voter has cast a valid vote without revealing their choice.
- Prevents double voting while maintaining voter anonymity.

4. Decentralized Finance (DeFi) Privacy Enhancements

- DeFi applications often lack privacy, exposing financial data.
- ZKPs enable private lending, borrowing, and trading on blockchain.

5. Enterprise and Government Use Cases

- Secure data sharing among enterprises without leaking sensitive information.
- Governments can conduct audits and compliance checks without accessing raw data.

Implementation of Zero-Knowledge Proofs in Blockchain

SEVERAL BLOCKCHAIN platforms have integrated ZKPs to improve privacy and security. Below are some notable implementations:

1. Zcash (zk-SNARKs)

- One of the first major blockchain projects to implement zk-SNARKs.

- Supports shielded transactions where sender, receiver, and amount remain confidential.

2. Ethereum zk-Rollups

- Ethereum is integrating zk-SNARKs and zk-STARKs for Layer 2 scaling solutions.

- zk-Rollups bundle multiple transactions into a single proof, reducing gas fees.

3. Aztec Protocol

- Enhances privacy in Ethereum-based transactions.

- Implements zk-SNARKs to enable confidential DeFi transactions.

4. StarkWare (zk-STARKs)

- Provides scalable and transparent zero-knowledge proofs.

- Used in applications like StarkEx and StarkNet to improve Ethereum scalability.

Sample zk-SNARK Implementation

A BASIC IMPLEMENTATION of zk-SNARKs in Solidity involves integrating a zero-knowledge proof system into a smart contract. Below is a simplified example using the **ZoKrates** toolkit.

```
pragma solidity ^0.8.0;

contract ZKProof {

event Verified(address indexed user);

function verifyProof(

uint[2] memory a,

uint[2][2] memory b,

uint[2] memory c,

uint[1] memory input

) public returns (bool) {

if (verify(a, b, c, input)) {

emit Verified(msg.sender);

return true;

}

return false;

}

function verify(

uint[2] memory a,
```

```
uint[2][2] memory b,
uint[2] memory c,
uint[1] memory input
) internal pure returns (bool) {
// zk-SNARK verification logic
return true; // Placeholder
}
}
```

This contract allows users to submit a zero-knowledge proof, and if valid, an event is emitted to confirm verification.

Challenges and Future of Zero-Knowledge Proofs

DESPITE THEIR ADVANTAGES, zero-knowledge proofs face several challenges:

- **Computational Complexity** – ZKP generation and verification require significant computational power.
- **Trusted Setup** – zk-SNARKs require an initial trusted setup, which can be a security risk.
- **Scalability Concerns** – Large-scale adoption of ZKPs requires optimization for performance.
- **Regulatory Considerations** – Governments and regulators may challenge privacy-centric applications.

Future Advancements in ZKPs

- **Post-Quantum Security** – zk-STARKs offer enhanced resistance against quantum computing threats.
- **Decentralized Identity Solutions** – ZKPs will play a crucial role in Web3 identity management.
- **Improved Efficiency** – Ongoing research focuses on reducing proof sizes and verification time.

Conclusion

ZERO-KNOWLEDGE PROOFS represent a breakthrough in cryptographic privacy and security. By enabling verifiable transactions without disclosing sensitive data, ZKPs enhance confidentiality across blockchain applications. From private transactions to secure identity verification, the potential of ZKPs is vast. As research and development continue, zero-knowledge proofs will play an increasingly vital role in the evolution of blockchain technology and Web3 privacy solutions.

AI and Blockchain Integration

Introduction

THE CONVERGENCE OF **Artificial Intelligence (AI) and Blockchain** is revolutionizing multiple industries by combining the strengths of decentralized, tamper-proof ledgers with the intelligence of machine learning and automation. AI provides blockchain with advanced data processing capabilities, predictive analytics, and automation, while blockchain enhances AI with trust, transparency, and security.

The integration of AI and blockchain can address key challenges in **data privacy, verifiability, security, and automation**. This fusion unlocks new possibilities in decentralized finance (DeFi), healthcare, supply chain management, identity verification, and more.

This section explores the relationship between AI and blockchain, key integration areas, real-world use cases, technical implementations, and the challenges that need to be addressed for widespread adoption.

The Synergy Between AI and Blockchain

AI AND BLOCKCHAIN HAVE distinct yet complementary properties:

- **Blockchain** provides **immutability, transparency, security, and decentralization**.

- **AI** offers **intelligence, automation, decision-making, and predictive capabilities**.

Integrating AI and blockchain can help in multiple ways:

- **Trustworthy AI**: Blockchain records AI model decisions, ensuring verifiability.

- **Secure Data Exchange**: Decentralized storage solutions protect AI training data.

- **Efficient Smart Contracts**: AI optimizes and automates complex contract executions.

- **Fraud Detection**: AI-driven analytics can identify fraudulent blockchain transactions.

Key Areas of AI-Blockchain Integration

1. Decentralized AI Marketplaces

- Traditional AI models are controlled by centralized tech giants.
- Blockchain enables decentralized AI model sharing, training, and execution.
- Example: **SingularityNET**, a blockchain-based AI marketplace that allows AI models to interact in a decentralized manner.

2. AI-Enhanced Smart Contracts

- Smart contracts currently operate on predefined logic.
- AI-powered smart contracts can adapt based on real-time data.
- Use Case: AI-driven **risk assessment in insurance** to adjust policies dynamically.

3. Secure and Transparent AI Models

- AI models trained on private datasets can be opaque and prone to bias.
- Storing AI model decisions on the blockchain ensures **auditability** and **bias detection**.
- Example: AI-generated medical diagnoses recorded on-chain for transparency.

4. Blockchain-Powered Federated Learning

- AI models need vast amounts of data, often stored in centralized repositories.

- **Federated learning** allows AI models to be trained across multiple decentralized data sources while preserving privacy.

- Blockchain ensures **tamper-proof data integrity** for federated learning models.

5. AI-Driven Blockchain Security

- AI algorithms detect malicious activities such as **51% attacks, Sybil attacks, and fraud**.

- Blockchain security protocols use AI for **intrusion detection and anomaly detection**.

- Example: AI-powered **fraud detection in crypto exchanges**.

6. Personalized AI in DeFi and Crypto Trading

- AI-driven bots analyze blockchain transactions for optimal investment decisions.

- Smart AI trading assistants predict **market trends** based on blockchain data.

- Example: AI-based **crypto trading bots** that leverage machine learning for market prediction.

Implementing AI in Blockchain: Technical Perspective

INTEGRATING AI WITH blockchain requires **on-chain** and **off-chain** approaches. Due to the limited computational capacity of smart contracts, AI models are usually run off-chain, with results recorded on-chain.

1. Off-Chain AI Computation with Blockchain Verification

- AI processes large datasets off-chain.
- Results are hashed and stored on the blockchain for verification.
- Example: AI-driven weather prediction for **blockchain-based crop insurance.**

2. AI-Powered Smart Contracts

- AI enhances **Ethereum smart contracts** using **oracles** to fetch real-time AI data.
- Use Case: A **predictive insurance contract** that adjusts premium rates dynamically based on AI risk assessments.

A BASIC SOLIDITY CONTRACT integrating AI-generated predictions:

```
pragma solidity ^0.8.0;

interface Oracle {

function getPrediction() external view returns (uint256);
```

```
}
contract AIInsurance {
address public oracleAddress;
uint256 public premium;
constructor(address _oracle) {
oracleAddress = _oracle;
}
function updatePremium() public {
uint256 riskFactor = Oracle(oracleAddress).getPrediction();
premium = riskFactor * 10; // Adjust premium based on AI prediction
}
function getPremium() public view returns (uint256) {
return premium;
}
}
```

3. Decentralized AI Training Using Blockchain Storage

- AI models require vast datasets, often stored on **IPFS, Arweave, or Filecoin.**
- Blockchain ensures **data provenance** and **trustworthiness.**

- Use Case: **AI-powered credit scoring** with decentralized financial data.

EXAMPLE OF AN **IPFS integration for AI dataset storage**:

```
const IPFS = require('ipfs-api');

const ipfs = IPFS({ host: 'ipfs.infura.io', port: 5001, protocol: 'https' });

async function storeAIModelData(data) {

let buffer = Buffer.from(JSON.stringify(data));

let result = await ipfs.add(buffer);

return result[0].hash; // Store this hash on blockchain

}
```

Real-World Use Cases of AI-Blockchain Integration

1. AI-Powered Fraud Detection in Finance

- AI analyzes blockchain transactions for anomalies.
- Fraudulent activities (e.g., money laundering) are flagged and recorded on-chain.

2. Blockchain-Based AI in Healthcare

- AI diagnoses diseases from medical images.
- Patient records stored securely on a blockchain for verification.

3. Decentralized AI for Identity Verification

- AI verifies users' identities without storing personal data in a centralized system.

- Example: **Self-sovereign identity** using AI-powered facial recognition.

4. AI-Driven Supply Chain Management

- AI tracks supply chain data stored on blockchain.

- Ensures **product authenticity** and **fraud prevention**.

5. AI-Powered DeFi Lending Protocols

- AI analyzes credit risk for blockchain-based lending platforms.

- Smart contracts adjust interest rates based on AI risk models.

Challenges in AI-Blockchain Integration

DESPITE THE POTENTIAL, there are challenges in integrating AI and blockchain:

1. **Computational Limitations** – AI models require intensive processing, which blockchain networks cannot handle natively.
2. **Scalability Issues** – Blockchain's consensus mechanisms can slow down AI-driven applications.
3. **Data Privacy Concerns** – AI requires large datasets, but sharing sensitive data on a public blockchain raises privacy

risks.

4. **Energy Consumption** – Both AI training and blockchain mining require significant computational power.
5. **Regulatory Barriers** – Governments may impose restrictions on AI-driven automated decision-making in blockchain.

Future Prospects

THE FUTURE OF AI AND blockchain integration looks promising with the emergence of:

- **AI-Oriented Layer 2 Solutions** – Enhancing computational efficiency for AI tasks.
- **Privacy-Preserving AI Models** – Using **zero-knowledge proofs (ZKPs)** for AI data processing.
- **Decentralized AI Training Networks** – AI models trained on **distributed computing networks**.
- **Autonomous DAOs with AI Governance** – AI-driven decision-making in **Decentralized Autonomous Organizations (DAOs)**.

Conclusion

AI AND BLOCKCHAIN INTEGRATION unlocks **new levels of security, transparency, and efficiency**. From AI-driven smart contracts to decentralized AI marketplaces, this convergence is reshaping multiple industries. While challenges remain in **scalability, privacy, and regulation**, advancements in **Layer 2 solutions, federated learning, and ZKPs** are paving the way for AI-powered blockchain ecosystems.

The fusion of AI and blockchain is set to drive the next wave of **decentralized automation, intelligent decision-making, and trustless computing**. As research and real-world implementations grow, this integration will define the future of **Web3, DeFi, healthcare, supply chains, and governance systems**.

The Future of Smart Contract Languages and Protocols

Introduction

AS BLOCKCHAIN TECHNOLOGY evolves, the need for more **efficient, secure, and scalable** smart contract languages and protocols becomes increasingly critical. The early adoption of **Solidity**, the most widely used smart contract language, has demonstrated both the power and limitations of smart contracts. Newer languages such as **Rust, Vyper, Move, and Cairo** are emerging to address issues related to **security, performance, and usability**.

In parallel, **next-generation smart contract protocols** are improving upon existing blockchain architectures to **enhance scalability, interoperability, and flexibility**. Layer 1 and Layer 2 solutions, along with novel consensus mechanisms, are reshaping the way smart contracts are deployed and executed.

This section explores the evolution of **smart contract languages**, key improvements in **next-gen protocols**, real-world applications, and the future trajectory of smart contract development.

Evolution of Smart Contract Languages

SMART CONTRACT LANGUAGES are the foundation of decentralized applications (DApps). As blockchain adoption grows, the **limitations of early smart contract languages** have become apparent, leading to the development of new languages designed to **enhance security, scalability, and efficiency**.

1. Solidity (Ethereum)

- The most widely used smart contract language.
- Based on JavaScript, C++, and Python.
- Vulnerable to **reentrancy attacks** and gas inefficiencies.
- Still dominates Ethereum and **EVM-compatible** blockchains.

A BASIC **Solidity** smart contract:

```
pragma solidity ^0.8.0;

contract SimpleStorage {

uint256 private data;

function set(uint256 _data) public {

data = _data;

}

function get() public view returns (uint256) {

return data;

}

}
```

2. Vyper (Ethereum Alternative)

- A more secure alternative to Solidity.
- Pythonic syntax with **readability and simplicity** as key design principles.
- Removes complex features such as inheritance to **reduce attack vectors.**

EXAMPLE OF **Vyper** code:

```
@public

def add(a: uint256, b: uint256) -> uint256:

return a + b
```

3. Rust (Solana, NEAR, Polkadot)

- A **memory-safe** and **performance-optimized** language.
- Used in **Solana, NEAR, and Polkadot smart contracts.**
- Prevents runtime vulnerabilities common in Solidity.

EXAMPLE OF A **Rust-based Solana smart contract**:

```
use solana_program::account_info::AccountInfo;

use solana_program::entrypoint::ProgramResult;

pub fn process_instruction(accounts: &[AccountInfo]) -> ProgramResult {
```

```
// Smart contract logic here
Ok(())
}
```

4. Move (Aptos, Sui)

- Developed by **Meta (formerly Facebook)** for the **Diem blockchain.**
- Focuses on **resource-based ownership** to prevent **double-spending attacks.**
- Designed for high-performance blockchains like **Aptos and Sui.**

EXAMPLE **Move smart contract:**

```
module MyModule {
struct Asset has key { value: u64 }
public fun create(value: u64): Asset {
return Asset { value };
}
}
```

5. Cairo (StarkNet)

- Designed for **zero-knowledge rollups (zk-Rollups).**
- Used in **StarkWare's Layer 2 scaling solutions.**

- Optimized for **computational efficiency** in **off-chain execution.**

A BASIC **Cairo contract:**

```
@view

func get_balance{syscall_ptr: felt*, pedersen_ptr: HashBuiltin*}() -> (balance: felt):

return (balance=1000)
```

Next-Generation Smart Contract Protocols

AS **Layer 1 and Layer 2 solutions** evolve, smart contract execution is being optimized for **scalability, security, and interoperability**.

1. Ethereum 2.0 and Optimistic Rollups

- Moves from **Proof of Work (PoW) to Proof of Stake (PoS).**
- Reduces gas fees and increases transaction throughput.
- **Optimistic Rollups** (e.g., **Optimism, Arbitrum**) scale Ethereum by executing transactions **off-chain.**

2. zk-Rollups and Zero-Knowledge Smart Contracts

- Zero-knowledge proofs (ZKPs) allow **privacy-preserving** smart contracts.
- **StarkNet and zkSync** implement **zk-Rollups** for efficient off-chain execution.

EXAMPLE: **zk-SNARKs verifying smart contract execution**

```
contract zkVerifier {
function verifyProof(
uint[2] memory a,
uint[2][2] memory b,
uint[2] memory c,
uint[1] memory input
) public pure returns (bool) {
return true; // Example verification logic
}
}
```

3. Polkadot and Cross-Chain Smart Contracts

- Enables **cross-chain interoperability** via **parachains.**
- Smart contracts on **Moonbeam (EVM-compatible parachain)** interact with multiple blockchains.

4. Cosmos and Inter-Blockchain Communication (IBC)

- Facilitates **interoperable smart contracts** across different blockchains.
- Smart contracts built using **CosmWasm** allow **cross-chain transactions.**

EXAMPLE OF A **CosmWasm smart contract** in Rust:

```
use cosmwasm_std::{to_binary, Binary, DepsMut};

pub fn execute(_deps: DepsMut) -> Result<Binary, String> {

Ok(to_binary("Hello, Cosmos!")?)

}
```

5. Aptos and Sui: High-Performance Smart Contracts

- Implements **parallel execution** to handle high transaction throughput.
- **Move language** ensures **better security** for smart contract execution.

Real-World Use Cases of Advanced Smart Contract Protocols

1. **Scalable DeFi Applications**

   ○ zk-Rollups reduce congestion in **decentralized exchanges (DEXs).**

   ○ Optimistic rollups enhance **lending and borrowing platforms.**

2. **Cross-Chain NFT Marketplaces**

   ○ **Polkadot and Cosmos IBC** enable multi-chain NFT trading.

   ○ Users can mint **NFTs on multiple blockchains.**

3. **Decentralized AI Marketplaces**

- **Ethereum zk-Rollups** power AI-generated content trading.
- AI models execute **privacy-preserving transactions** using **zk-SNARKs.**

4. **Enterprise-Grade Smart Contracts**

- **Hyperledger Fabric** allows businesses to deploy **permissioned smart contracts.**
- Used for **supply chain tracking, digital identities, and corporate governance.**

Challenges and Future Developments

DESPITE ADVANCEMENTS, smart contract development faces challenges:

- **Security Risks** – Solidity remains vulnerable to **reentrancy attacks.**
- **Gas Fees** – Ethereum contracts remain expensive compared to **Layer 2 solutions.**
- **Developer Learning Curve** – Newer languages like **Move and Cairo** require additional expertise.
- **Interoperability** – Standardized **cross-chain smart contract execution** is still under development.

Future improvements in **Ethereum 2.0, zk-Rollups, AI-powered smart contracts, and multi-chain interactions** will define the **next era of decentralized applications**.

Conclusion

THE FUTURE OF **smart contract languages and protocols** is centered around **efficiency, security, and scalability**. While **Solidity** remains dominant, newer languages such as **Move, Cairo, and Rust** are emerging to meet the needs of **next-generation decentralized applications**.

Protocols like **zk-Rollups, Optimistic Rollups, Cosmos IBC, and Polkadot parachains** are paving the way for **interoperable, scalable, and efficient smart contracts**. The evolution of **AI-driven smart contracts, zero-knowledge execution, and cross-chain frameworks** will further transform the landscape of **blockchain-based automation**.

As blockchain adoption grows, the **continuous innovation in smart contract languages and protocols** will be crucial in **shaping the decentralized future**.

Chapter 11: Appendices

Glossary of Terms

Address

A UNIQUE IDENTIFIER in blockchain, typically a string of alphanumeric characters, representing a wallet, smart contract, or another entity on the blockchain.

Airdrop

A DISTRIBUTION OF TOKENS or coins, usually free, to multiple wallet addresses as a marketing or reward strategy.

Block

A COLLECTION OF TRANSACTIONS grouped together and added to a blockchain. Blocks are verified and appended through a consensus mechanism.

Blockchain

A DECENTRALIZED, DISTRIBUTED ledger that records transactions across multiple computers in a secure and immutable way.

Block Explorer

AN ONLINE TOOL THAT allows users to view blockchain transactions, addresses, blocks, and other data.

Block Reward

THE INCENTIVE GIVEN to miners or validators for successfully adding a new block to the blockchain.

Consensus Mechanism

A METHOD USED BY BLOCKCHAIN networks to agree on the validity of transactions. Examples include Proof of Work (PoW) and Proof of Stake (PoS).

Cryptocurrency

A DIGITAL OR VIRTUAL currency that uses cryptographic techniques for security and operates independently of central authorities.

DAO (Decentralized Autonomous Organization)

AN ORGANIZATION THAT operates through smart contracts and is governed by token holders rather than a centralized entity.

DApp (Decentralized Application)

AN APPLICATION BUILT on a blockchain that operates without a central authority, often utilizing smart contracts.

DeFi (Decentralized Finance)

A FINANCIAL ECOSYSTEM built on blockchain that offers traditional financial services like lending, borrowing, and trading without intermediaries.

Double Spending

A PROBLEM IN DIGITAL currencies where a single token can be spent more than once. Blockchains solve this through consensus mechanisms.

EIP (Ethereum Improvement Proposal)

A FORMAL PROPOSAL FOR improvements or changes to Ethereum's protocol, reviewed and approved by the community.

EVM (Ethereum Virtual Machine)

THE RUNTIME ENVIRONMENT for executing smart contracts on Ethereum, enabling decentralized computation.

Fork

A SPLIT IN A BLOCKCHAIN network resulting from protocol changes. Hard forks create a separate chain, while soft forks remain compatible with older versions.

Gas

A UNIT THAT MEASURES the computational effort required to execute transactions and smart contracts on Ethereum.

Gas Fee

A FEE PAID BY USERS to compensate miners or validators for processing transactions on the blockchain.

Hash

A FIXED-LENGTH ALPHANUMERIC output generated by a cryptographic function, used to ensure data integrity and security.

Hash Rate

THE SPEED AT WHICH a blockchain miner completes an operation, typically measured in hashes per second.

ICO (Initial Coin Offering)

A FUNDRAISING METHOD where new cryptocurrencies or tokens are sold to investors before their official launch.

Interoperability

THE ABILITY OF DIFFERENT blockchain networks to communicate and interact with each other.

Layer 2 Scaling

SOLUTIONS BUILT ON top of a blockchain to improve scalability and reduce transaction fees, such as Rollups and Plasma.

Liquidity

THE EASE WITH WHICH an asset can be converted into cash or other assets without significantly affecting its price.

Mainnet

THE FULLY OPERATIONAL and live version of a blockchain network where real transactions occur.

Merkle Tree

A STRUCTURE USED TO efficiently verify blockchain data, ensuring transactions are secure and immutable.

Miner

A PARTICIPANT IN A Proof-of-Work blockchain who validates transactions and adds blocks to the network.

Mining

THE PROCESS OF USING computational power to validate and add transactions to a blockchain in Proof-of-Work networks.

NFT (Non-Fungible Token)

A UNIQUE DIGITAL ASSET representing ownership of a specific item, such as art, collectibles, or virtual real estate.

Node

A COMPUTER THAT MAINTAINS a copy of the blockchain and participates in the network's operations.

Off-Chain

TRANSACTIONS OR DATA storage that occur outside of the blockchain to improve efficiency and scalability.

On-Chain

TRANSACTIONS OR ACTIVITIES that take place directly on the blockchain and are recorded immutably.

Oracle

A SERVICE THAT FETCHES external data (e.g., weather, stock prices) and provides it to smart contracts.

P2P (Peer-to-Peer)

A DECENTRALIZED NETWORK structure where participants interact directly without intermediaries.

Private Key

A SECRET CRYPTOGRAPHIC key used to sign transactions and prove ownership of blockchain assets.

Proof of Stake (PoS)

A CONSENSUS MECHANISM where validators are selected based on the amount of cryptocurrency they hold and stake.

Proof of Work (PoW)

A CONSENSUS MECHANISM requiring computational work (mining) to validate transactions and secure the blockchain.

Public Key

A CRYPTOGRAPHIC KEY derived from a private key, used to receive transactions and verify signatures.

Rug Pull

A FRAUDULENT PRACTICE where developers abandon a project after collecting funds from investors.

Satoshi

THE SMALLEST UNIT OF Bitcoin, equivalent to 0.00000001 BTC.

Smart Contract

A SELF-EXECUTING CONTRACT with terms directly written into code, running on a blockchain.

Testnet

A BLOCKCHAIN NETWORK used for testing and development before deploying to the mainnet.

Token

A DIGITAL ASSET BUILT on a blockchain that represents value, utility, or governance rights.

Tokenomics

THE ECONOMIC MODEL and supply mechanisms of a cryptocurrency or token.

Validator

A PARTICIPANT IN A Proof-of-Stake network who validates transactions and secures the blockchain.

Wallet

A SOFTWARE OR HARDWARE tool that allows users to store, send, and receive cryptocurrencies.

Web3

A DECENTRALIZED VERSION of the internet that integrates blockchain, smart contracts, and peer-to-peer interactions.

Zero-Knowledge Proof

A CRYPTOGRAPHIC TECHNIQUE that allows one party to prove knowledge of information without revealing the information itself.

Resources for Further Learning

Books

1. **Mastering Blockchain** – *Imran Bashir*
   A comprehensive guide covering blockchain technology, cryptography, and smart contracts.
2. **Blockchain Basics** – *Daniel Drescher*
   A non-technical introduction to blockchain, explaining key concepts in 25 easy steps.
3. **Ethereum for Web Developers** – *Bruno Skvorc*
   A practical guide to building decentralized applications (DApps) on Ethereum.
4. **The Infinite Machine** – *Camila Russo*
   A historical account of the creation of Ethereum and the people behind it.
5. **Blockchain Revolution** – *Don Tapscott & Alex Tapscott*
   Discusses the impact of blockchain technology on the future of business and society.

Online Courses

1. **Blockchain Specialization – University at Buffalo (Coursera)**
   Covers blockchain fundamentals, smart contracts, and decentralized applications.
2. **Ethereum and Solidity: The Complete Developer's**

Guide – Udemy
A hands-on course that teaches Ethereum smart contract development using Solidity.

3. **Certified Blockchain Developer – Blockchain Council**
An in-depth certification program focusing on blockchain development.
4. **CS251: Bitcoin and Cryptocurrencies – Stanford University**
A university-level course exploring the technical foundations of Bitcoin and blockchain.
5. **Ethereum Smart Contract Development – ConsenSys Academy**
A professional training program for building secure and efficient Ethereum applications.

Developer Documentation

1. **Ethereum Developer Documentation** – ethereum.org/developers
Official documentation covering Solidity, Web3.js, and Ethereum development tools.
2. **Solidity Documentation** –soliditylang.org
[6] The official guide for learning and mastering Solidity programming.
3. **Web3.js Documentation** –web3js.readthedocs.io
[7] A comprehensive reference for interacting with Ethereum blockchain using Web3.js.
4. **Hardhat Documentation** –hardhat.org
[8] Guides for setting up and using Hardhat, a popular

6. https://soliditylang.org/
7. https://web3js.readthedocs.io/
8. https://hardhat.org/

Ethereum development environment.

5. **Truffle Suite Documentation** – trufflesuite.com/docs Explains how to develop, test, and deploy smart contracts using Truffle.

Popular Blockchain Communities

1. **Ethereum Stack Exchange** –ethereum.stackexchange.com[9]

A Q&A site dedicated to Ethereum development and related blockchain topics.

2. **r/ethereum on Reddit** –reddit.com/r/ethereum[10]

A discussion forum for Ethereum news, projects, and community discussions.

3. **Discord Blockchain Communities**

○ Ethereum Developers: discord.gg/ethereum

○ Solidity Developers: discord.gg/solidity

○ Web3 Developers: discord.gg/web3

4. **Bitcoin Talk Forum** –bitcointalk.org[11]

One of the oldest blockchain communities discussing Bitcoin and cryptocurrency.

5. **GitHub Blockchain Repositories**

---

9. https://ethereum.stackexchange.com/

10. https://www.reddit.com/r/ethereum/

11. https://bitcointalk.org/

- Ethereum:github.com/ethereum[12]
- Solidity:github.com/ethereum/solidity[13]
- Web3.js:github.com/ChainSafe/web3.js[14]

Blockchain Research Papers and Whitepapers

1. **Bitcoin Whitepaper – Satoshi Nakamoto**
Bitcoin: A Peer-to-Peer Electronic Cash System
bitcoin.org/bitcoin.pdf
2. **Ethereum Whitepaper – Vitalik Buterin**
Ethereum: A Next-Generation Smart Contract and Decentralized Application Platform
ethereum.org/en/whitepaper
3. **Polkadot Whitepaper – Gavin Wood**
Polkadot: Vision for a Heterogeneous Multi-Chain Framework
polkadot.network/whitepaper
4. **Zcash: Privacy-Protecting Digital Currency**
Zero-Knowledge Proofs and Privacy in Cryptocurrency
z.cash/technology
5. **Libra (Diem) Whitepaper**
Libra Blockchain: A New Decentralized Financial Infrastructure
libra.org/en-US/white-paper

Tools for Smart Contract Development

1. **Remix IDE** – remix.ethereum.org

12. https://github.com/ethereum

13. https://github.com/ethereum/solidity

14. https://github.com/ChainSafe/web3.js

A browser-based IDE for writing, testing, and deploying Solidity smart contracts.

2. **Ganache** – trufflesuite.com/ganache
   A personal Ethereum blockchain for local development and testing.
3. **Infura** –infura.io
   [15] A blockchain infrastructure provider for connecting DApps to Ethereum nodes.
4. **Alchemy** –alchemy.com
   [16] A blockchain development platform that offers high-performance API services.
5. **Ethers.js** – docs.ethers.io
   A JavaScript library for interacting with Ethereum and smart contracts.

Security and Audit Resources

1. **OpenZeppelin** –openzeppelin.com
   [17] A leading security firm providing smart contract security solutions and libraries.
2. **CertiK** –certik.com
   [18] A blockchain security firm specializing in smart contract audits.
3. **Slither** –github.com/crytic/slither
   [19] A static analysis tool for detecting vulnerabilities in Solidity contracts.
4. **MythX** –mythx.io

---

15. https://infura.io/
16. https://www.alchemy.com/
17. https://openzeppelin.com/
18. https://www.certik.com/
19. https://github.com/crytic/slither

[20] A security analysis service for detecting smart contract vulnerabilities.

5. **DASP Top 10** –dasp.co
   [21] A list of the top 10 smart contract vulnerabilities to watch out for.

Web3 and Blockchain Development Blogs

1. **Ethereum Foundation Blog** – blog.ethereum.org
   Official blog covering Ethereum upgrades, research, and community initiatives.
2. **ConsenSys Blog** – consensys.net/blog
   Insights on Ethereum, smart contract development, and blockchain trends.
3. **Hackernoon Blockchain Stories** – hackernoon.com/tagged/blockchain
   Articles and tutorials on blockchain development and decentralization.
4. **CoinDesk Developer Section** – coindesk.com/developers
   News and resources for blockchain and crypto developers.
5. **Web3 Foundation Blog** – web3.foundation/blog
   Research and developments in Web3 and decentralized technologies.

Conferences and Hackathons

1. **ETHGlobal** –ethglobal.com
   [22] A global series of Ethereum hackathons where developers build innovative DApps.
2. **Devcon** –devcon.org

20. https://mythx.io/

21. https://dasp.co/

22. https://ethglobal.com/

[23] The annual Ethereum developer conference hosted by the Ethereum Foundation.

3. **Consensus by CoinDesk** – coindesk.com/events/consensus
   One of the largest blockchain conferences featuring industry leaders.
4. **Polkadot Decoded** – polkadot.network/events
   A conference dedicated to Polkadot's blockchain ecosystem.
5. **Solana Breakpoint** – solana.com/breakpoint
   A yearly conference highlighting Solana blockchain innovations.

BY LEVERAGING THESE resources, developers, researchers, and enthusiasts can stay updated on blockchain advancements, enhance their skills, and contribute to the growth of the decentralized ecosystem.

Sample Projects and Code Snippets

Introduction

THIS SECTION PROVIDES hands-on sample projects and code snippets to help developers understand and implement key concepts in decentralized application (DApp) development. The projects range from basic smart contracts to full-stack DApps, including backend integration and frontend development.

23. https://devcon.org/

Project 1: Basic Solidity Smart Contract (Hello Blockchain)

A SIMPLE SMART CONTRACT written in Solidity that stores and retrieves a message.

1.1 Setting Up the Environment

BEFORE WRITING THE contract, ensure that you have Solidity installed. You can use **Remix IDE** or a local environment with **Hardhat**.

To install Hardhat, use the following command:

npm install—save-dev hardhat

Initialize a Hardhat project:

npx hardhat

Choose "Create a basic sample project" and install dependencies.

1.2 Writing the Smart Contract

CREATE A NEW SOLIDITY file HelloBlockchain.sol inside the contracts/ folder.

// SPDX-License-Identifier: MIT

pragma solidity ^0.8.0;

contract HelloBlockchain {

string private message;

event MessageUpdated(string oldMessage, string newMessage);

constructor(string memory initialMessage) {

```
message = initialMessage;

}

function getMessage() public view returns (string memory) {

return message;

}

function setMessage(string memory newMessage) public {

string memory oldMessage = message;

message = newMessage;

emit MessageUpdated(oldMessage, newMessage);

}

}
```

1.3 Deploying the Contract

CREATE A NEW DEPLOYMENT script deploy.js in the scripts/ folder.

```
const hre = require("hardhat");

async function main() {

const HelloBlockchain = await hre.ethers.getContractFactory("HelloBlockchain");

const hello = await HelloBlockchain.deploy("Hello, Blockchain!");

await hello.deployed();

console.log("Contract deployed to:", hello.address);
```

```
}
main()
.then(() => process.exit(0))
.catch((error) => {
console.error(error);
process.exit(1);
});
```

Run the deployment:

```
npx hardhat run scripts/deploy.js—network localhost
```

Project 2: Decentralized To-Do List DApp

A BASIC TO-DO LIST application where users can add, complete, and remove tasks on the Ethereum blockchain.

2.1 Smart Contract for To-Do List

CREATE TODO.SOL IN the contracts/ folder.

```
// SPDX-License-Identifier: MIT
pragma solidity ^0.8.0;
contract ToDoList {
struct Task {
uint id;
string content;
```

```
bool completed;
}
mapping(uint => Task) public tasks;
uint public taskCount;
event TaskCreated(uint id, string content);
event TaskCompleted(uint id, bool completed);
function createTask(string memory content) public {
taskCount++;
tasks[taskCount] = Task(taskCount, content, false);
emit TaskCreated(taskCount, content);
}
function completeTask(uint id) public {
tasks[id].completed = true;
emit TaskCompleted(id, true);
}
}
```

2.2 Frontend with React and Web3.js

CREATE A SIMPLE REACT frontend to interact with the smart contract.

Install dependencies:

```
npm install ethers web3
```

Create a React component ToDoList.js:

```
import React, { useEffect, useState } from "react";

import { ethers } from "ethers";

import ToDoListABI from "./ToDoList.json";

const contractAddress = "YOUR_CONTRACT_ADDRESS_HERE";

const ToDoList = () => {

const [tasks, setTasks] = useState([]);

const [taskContent, setTaskContent] = useState("");

const [provider, setProvider] = useState(null);

const [contract, setContract] = useState(null);

useEffect(() => {

const initBlockchain = async () => {

const web3Provider = new ethers.providers.Web3Provider(window.ethereum);

const signer = web3Provider.getSigner();

const todoContract = new ethers.Contract(contractAddress, ToDoListABI, signer);

setProvider(web3Provider);

setContract(todoContract);
```

```
const taskCount = await todoContract.taskCount();

let tasksArray = [];

for (let i = 1; i <= taskCount; i++) {

const task = await todoContract.tasks(i);

tasksArray.push({ id: task.id.toNumber(), content: task.content,
completed: task.completed });

}

setTasks(tasksArray);

};

initBlockchain();

}, []);

const createTask = async () => {

const tx = await contract.createTask(taskContent);

await tx.wait();

window.location.reload();

};

const completeTask = async (id) => {

const tx = await contract.completeTask(id);

await tx.wait();

window.location.reload();

};
```

```
return (

<div>

<h2>Blockchain To-Do List</h2>

<input type="text" value={taskContent} onChange={(e) =>
setTaskContent(e.target.value)} />

<button onClick={createTask}>Add Task</button>

<ul>

{tasks.map((task) => (

<li key={task.id}>

{task.content} {task.completed ? "✔" : ""}

{!task.completed && <button onClick={() =>
completeTask(task.id)}>Complete</button>}

</li>

))}

</ul>

</div>

);

};

export default ToDoList;
```

Project 3: NFT Marketplace Smart Contract

THIS IS A BASIC NFT marketplace contract where users can mint and list NFTs for sale.

3.1 Smart Contract

CREATE NFTMARKETPLACE.sol in the contracts/ folder.

```
// SPDX-License-Identifier: MIT

pragma solidity ^0.8.0;

import "@openzeppelin/contracts/token/ERC721/extensions/ERC721URIStorage.sol";

import "@openzeppelin/contracts/access/Ownable.sol";

contract NFTMarketplace is ERC721URIStorage, Ownable {

uint256 public tokenCounter;

constructor() ERC721("NFTMarketplace", "NFTM") {

tokenCounter = 0;

}

function createNFT(string memory tokenURI) public onlyOwner {

uint256 newTokenId = tokenCounter;

_mint(msg.sender, newTokenId);

_setTokenURI(newTokenId, tokenURI);

tokenCounter++;

}
```

```
}
```

3.2 Deploying and Testing the NFT Marketplace

MODIFY DEPLOY.JS:

```
const hre = require("hardhat");

async function main() {

const NFTMarketplace = await hre.ethers.getContractFactory("NFTMarketplace");

const nftMarketplace = await NFTMarketplace.deploy();

await nftMarketplace.deployed();

console.log("NFT Marketplace deployed at:", nftMarketplace.address);

}

main()

.then(() => process.exit(0))

.catch((error) => {

console.error(error);

process.exit(1);

});
```

Deploy with:

```
npx hardhat run scripts/deploy.js—network localhost
```

Conclusion

THESE PROJECTS INTRODUCE core concepts of Solidity, smart contract deployment, and frontend integration using Web3.js and React. Developers can expand on these by adding features such as payments, user authentication, and advanced UI designs to create real-world DApps.

API Reference Guide

Introduction

THIS SECTION PROVIDES an extensive API reference for common blockchain and Web3 development frameworks, focusing on **Ethereum**, **Solidity**, **Web3.js**, **Ethers.js**, and **IPFS**. The guide includes method definitions, usage examples, and best practices to facilitate the development of decentralized applications (DApps).

---

1. Solidity Smart Contract Functions

SOLIDITY IS THE PRIMARY programming language for writing Ethereum smart contracts. Below are essential functions used in contract development.

1.1 Basic Contract Structure

A SIMPLE SOLIDITY CONTRACT includes state variables, constructors, and functions.

```
// SPDX-License-Identifier: MIT

pragma solidity ^0.8.0;

contract SimpleContract {
```

```
string public message;

constructor(string memory initialMessage) {

message = initialMessage;

}

function setMessage(string memory newMessage) public {

message = newMessage;

}

function getMessage() public view returns (string memory) {

return message;

}

}
```

1.2 Common Solidity Functions

- **msg.sender** – Retrieves the caller of the function.
- **msg.value** – Retrieves the amount of Ether sent with a function call.
- **require()** – Ensures a condition is met; otherwise, it reverts.
- **emit** – Triggers an event.

EXAMPLE:

```
function sendEther() public payable {

require(msg.value > 0, "Send some Ether");
```

emit PaymentReceived(msg.sender, msg.value);

}

1.3 Events and Logging

EVENTS ALLOW LOGGING of contract actions.

event PaymentReceived(address indexed sender, uint amount);

Emitting an event:

emit PaymentReceived(msg.sender, msg.value);

---

2. Web3.js API Reference

WEB3.JS IS A JAVASCRIPT library for interacting with Ethereum nodes.

2.1 Connecting to Ethereum

CONST WEB3 = REQUIRE("web3");

const web3 = new Web3("https://mainnet.infura.io/v3/YOUR_INFURA_PROJECT_ID");

2.2 Retrieving an Ethereum Account Balance

ASYNC FUNCTION GETBALANCE(address) {

const balance = await web3.eth.getBalance(address);

console.log("Balance:", web3.utils.fromWei(balance, "ether"), "ETH");

}

```
getBalance("0x742d35Cc6634C0532925a3b844Bc454e4438f44e");
```

2.3 Sending Ether

```
ASYNC FUNCTION SENDTRANSACTION(from, to, amount) {

const tx = {

from,

to,

value: web3.utils.toWei(amount, "ether"),

gas: 21000,

};

const signedTx = await web3.eth.accounts.signTransaction(tx, "YOUR_PRIVATE_KEY");

const receipt = await web3.eth.sendSignedTransaction(signedTx.rawTransaction);

console.log("Transaction Hash:", receipt.transactionHash);

}
```

3. Ethers.js API Reference

ETHERS.JS IS A LIGHTWEIGHT alternative to Web3.js for interacting with Ethereum.

3.1 Connecting to Ethereum

```
CONST { ETHERS } = require("ethers");
```

const provider = new ethers.providers.JsonRpcProvider("https://mainnet.infura.io/v3/YOUR_INFURA_PROJECT_ID");

3.2 Reading a Smart Contract

CONST CONTRACTADDRESS = "0xYourContractAddress";

const abi = [...]; // Your contract ABI

const contract = new ethers.Contract(contractAddress, abi, provider);

async function getValue() {

const value = await contract.getMessage();

console.log("Stored Value:", value);

}

getValue();

3.3 Writing to a Smart Contract

CONST WALLET = NEW ethers.Wallet("YOUR_PRIVATE_KEY", provider);

const contractWithSigner = contract.connect(wallet);

async function setValue(newMessage) {

const tx = await contractWithSigner.setMessage(newMessage);

await tx.wait();

console.log("Message updated.");

```
}

setValue("Hello, Blockchain!");
```

4. IPFS API Reference

IPFS (INTERPLANETARY File System) is a decentralized file storage network.

4.1 Installing IPFS

```
NPM INSTALL IPFS-HTTP-client
```

4.2 Uploading a File to IPFS

```
CONST IPFSCLIENT = require("ipfs-http-client");

const ipfs = ipfsClient.create({ host: "ipfs.infura.io", port: 5001, protocol: "https" });

async function uploadFile(fileContent) {

const { path } = await ipfs.add(fileContent);

console.log("File uploaded at:", path);

}

uploadFile("Hello, IPFS!");
```

4.3 Retrieving a File from IPFS

```
ASYNC FUNCTION FETCHFILE(cid) {

const stream = ipfs.cat(cid);

let data = "";
```

```
for await (const chunk of stream) {
data += chunk.toString();
}
console.log("File Content:", data);
}
fetchFile("QmYourFileHash");
```

5. Blockchain Query APIs

SEVERAL APIS PROVIDE blockchain data access:

5.1 TheGraph API

THEGRAPH ALLOWS QUERYING blockchain data with GraphQL.

Example query to fetch ERC-20 token transfers:

```
{
transfers(first: 5, where: { from: "0xAddress" }) {
id
from
to
value
}
}
```

5.2 Infura API

INFURA PROVIDES ETHEREUM and IPFS infrastructure.

Retrieve the latest Ethereum block:

```
const latestBlock = await provider.getBlockNumber();

console.log("Latest Block:", latestBlock);
```

5.3 Alchemy API

ALCHEMY OFFERS ENHANCED blockchain data services.

Fetch gas price:

```
const gasPrice = await provider.getGasPrice();

console.log("Gas Price:", ethers.utils.formatUnits(gasPrice, "gwei"), "Gwei");
```

6. Best Practices for Using APIs

6.1 Rate Limiting and Caching

- Many APIs impose request limits; use **batch requests** or **caching**.
- Example: Cache Ethereum prices using Redis.

6.2 Security Considerations

- Never expose private keys in front-end applications.
- Use **.env** files to store sensitive data:

```
INFURA_API_KEY=YOUR_infura_key
```

PRIVATE_KEY=your_private_key

6.3 Handling API Errors

EXAMPLE OF HANDLING transaction errors:

```
try {

const tx = await contract.setValue("New Value");

await tx.wait();

} catch (error) {

console.error("Transaction failed:", error);

}
```

Conclusion

THIS API REFERENCE Guide serves as a foundational resource for blockchain developers. It covers Solidity smart contracts, Web3.js, Ethers.js, IPFS, and key blockchain data APIs. Developers can leverage these tools to build scalable, decentralized applications with robust backend and frontend integrations.

Frequently Asked Questions

General Blockchain Questions

What is blockchain?

BLOCKCHAIN IS A DECENTRALIZED, distributed ledger technology that records transactions across multiple computers in a secure and immutable manner. It ensures transparency, security, and trust in digital interactions without the need for intermediaries.

What are the different types of blockchains?

THERE ARE THREE PRIMARY types of blockchains:

- **Public Blockchains** – Open to everyone (e.g., Bitcoin, Ethereum).
- **Private Blockchains** – Restricted access for selected participants (e.g., Hyperledger).
- **Consortium Blockchains** – Controlled by multiple organizations (e.g., Quorum).

How does blockchain achieve consensus?

BLOCKCHAINS USE DIFFERENT consensus mechanisms, such as:

- **Proof of Work (PoW)** – Miners solve cryptographic puzzles (e.g., Bitcoin).
- **Proof of Stake (PoS)** – Validators are chosen based on token holdings (e.g., Ethereum 2.0).
- **Delegated Proof of Stake (DPoS)** – Users vote for trusted validators (e.g., EOS).
- **Practical Byzantine Fault Tolerance (PBFT)** – Nodes agree on a transaction state (e.g., Hyperledger Fabric).

What is a smart contract?

A SMART CONTRACT IS a self-executing contract with the terms directly written in code. It runs on the blockchain and automatically enforces agreements without intermediaries.

What are gas fees in Ethereum?

GAS FEES ARE TRANSACTION fees paid to miners or validators for executing smart contracts and processing transactions. Gas is measured in **Gwei**, a fraction of **ETH**.

Example of checking gas prices using Web3.js:

```
const gasPrice = await web3.eth.getGasPrice();

console.log("Gas Price:", web3.utils.fromWei(gasPrice, "gwei"), "Gwei");
```

Development and Smart Contract Questions

How do I write a basic smart contract in Solidity?

HERE'S AN EXAMPLE OF a simple **Hello World** smart contract:

```
// SPDX-License-Identifier: MIT

pragma solidity ^0.8.0;

contract HelloWorld {

string public message;

constructor(string memory initialMessage) {

message = initialMessage;
```

}

function setMessage(string memory newMessage) public {

message = newMessage;

}

}

How do I deploy a smart contract?

USING **Hardhat**, follow these steps:

Install Hardhat:

bash

npm install—save-dev hardhat

1.

Create a new project:

bash

npx hardhat

1.

Compile the contract:

bash

npx hardhat compile

1.

Deploy using a script:

javascript

```
const hre = require("hardhat");

async function main() {

const Contract = await hre.ethers.getContractFactory("HelloWorld");

const contract = await Contract.deploy("Hello, Blockchain!");

await contract.deployed();

console.log("Contract deployed at:", contract.address);

}

main().catch((error) => {

console.error(error);

process.exit(1);

});
```

1.

Run the deployment script:

bash

```
npx hardhat run scripts/deploy.js—network localhost
```

1.

DApp Development Questions

How do I connect a DApp to Ethereum?

USE **Web3.js** or **Ethers.js** to interact with the Ethereum blockchain.

Example using **Ethers.js**:

```
const { ethers } = require("ethers");

const provider = new ethers.providers.JsonRpcProvider("https://mainnet.infura.io/v3/YOUR_INFURA_PROJECT_ID");
```

How do I integrate MetaMask with a DApp?

```
ASYNC FUNCTION CONNECTMETAMASK() {

if (window.ethereum) {

await window.ethereum.request({ method: "eth_requestAccounts" });

console.log("Connected:", window.ethereum.selectedAddress);

} else {

console.log("MetaMask not detected!");

}

}
```

What is an ERC-20 token, and how do I create one?

AN ERC-20 TOKEN IS a **fungible** token standard on Ethereum.

Here's a basic ERC-20 contract:

```
// SPDX-License-Identifier: MIT
pragma solidity ^0.8.0;
import "@openzeppelin/contracts/token/ERC20/ERC20.sol";
contract MyToken is ERC20 {
constructor(uint256 initialSupply) ERC20("MyToken", "MTK") {
_mint(msg.sender, initialSupply);
}
}
```

Security and Best Practices Questions

How do I secure my smart contract?

- Use **OpenZeppelin Contracts** for standard implementations.
- Implement **require()** and **revert()** to handle invalid inputs.
- Conduct **security audits** using tools like **Slither** or **MythX**.

EXAMPLE OF A **reentrancy attack** prevention mechanism:

```
mapping(address => uint) balances;
function withdraw(uint amount) public {
```

```
require(balances[msg.sender] >= amount, "Insufficient balance");

// Update balance before external call

balances[msg.sender] -= amount;

(bool success, ) = msg.sender.call{value: amount}("");

require(success, "Transfer failed");

}
```

What are the most common vulnerabilities in smart contracts?

- **Reentrancy Attacks** – External calls before updating internal state.
- **Integer Overflows/Underflows** – Use **SafeMath** or Solidity ^0.8.0 (built-in checks).
- **Front-Running** – Use commit-reveal schemes or private transactions.
- **Phishing Attacks** – Always verify contract addresses before transactions.

Ethereum Network and Gas Questions

Why are Ethereum gas fees so high?

GAS FEES DEPEND ON **network congestion** and the complexity of transactions.

Use **Layer 2 solutions** (e.g., **Polygon, Optimism**) to reduce costs.

How can I check the gas price before sending a transaction?

```
CONST GASPRICE = AWAIT provider.getGasPrice();

console.log("Current Gas Price:", ethers.utils.formatUnits(gasPrice, "gwei"), "Gwei");
```

How do I interact with a deployed contract?

USING **Ethers.js**, first connect to a contract:

```
const contract = new ethers.Contract(contractAddress, contractABI, signer);
```

Then call a **read function**:

```
const value = await contract.getMessage();

console.log("Stored Value:", value);
```

And execute a **write function**:

```
const tx = await contract.setMessage("New Message");

await tx.wait();

console.log("Transaction confirmed!");
```

NFT and Web3 Questions

How do I mint an NFT?

USING SOLIDITY:

```
contract MyNFT is ERC721 {
```

```
uint256 public tokenCounter;

constructor() ERC721("MyNFT", "MNFT") {

tokenCounter = 0;

}

function mintNFT(address recipient) public {

_safeMint(recipient, tokenCounter);

tokenCounter++;

}

}
```

How do I list an NFT on OpenSea?

- Deploy the **ERC-721** contract.
- Register the contract on **OpenSea**.
- Use **IPFS** to store NFT metadata.

What is Web3?

WEB3 REFERS TO A **decentralized internet** where users control their own data. It leverages **blockchain, smart contracts, and decentralized storage.**

Conclusion

THIS FAQ COVERS ESSENTIAL blockchain concepts, development strategies, and security best practices. Whether you're a beginner or an advanced developer, understanding these topics will help you build, deploy, and secure decentralized applications effectively.

www.ingramcontent.com/pod-product-compliance
Lightning Source LLC
LaVergne TN
LVHW090259210926
848480LV00001B/78